'This book gives a solid bibli
think about the eternal valu
God's good earth. Cosden lu
experience between the churc
less than biblical valuation o
grounds his alternative theological proposal in Scripture. His twin explorations of the implications of the Christ's resurrection and the foundations of human culture in Genesis 1-11 lead Cosden to claim that even the "work of our hands" may be redeemed and continue into eternity as part of the new heavens and new earth that God has in store. This is an important, clearly written book.'

J. Richard Middleton, Associate Professor of Biblical Studies, Roberts Wesleyan College

'It's taken too long for theologians to finally explain how what you do for a daily living is important in God's eyes. At last Darrell Cosden has done it. Bringing together the greats of Protestant and Catholic theology with contemporary theological developments and relevant elements of the Bible, Cosden produces a well-reasoned and heartfelt argument that ordinary work is ultimately important because it survives into eternity. The work you do – engineering, digging ditches, sculpting, serving food, making computer chips – is of eternal significance, or at least it could be. Surprising, substantial, thoroughly informed, clear, and readable for ordinary workers whose work may turn out be less ordinary than they think, The Heavenly Good of Earthly Work emerges as a premier resource for understanding work in Christian perspective.'

William Messenger, Director of the Mockler Center for Faith and Ethics in the Workplace, Gordon-Conwell Theological Seminary

'Darrell Cosden tackles the subject of work and its ultimate meaning and purpose, and he does so very wisely: by going deep into theology, and deep into the Bible. When we finish the book, we find not only that our thinking about work has been transformed, but also that our understanding of the Christian message has been immeasurably enriched. Highly recommended!'

Brian McLaren, pastor, author and activist (anewkindofchristian.com)

'This is cutting-edge theology of the highest order. Darrell Cosden's proposal for a new theology of work, based on careful exposition of key biblical passages, makes a vital contribution to the ongoing search for a new paradigm of the Christian mission in the twenty-first century. This might be described as a theology of liberation for the middle classes since this engagingly written book possesses the potential to transform our views of work, worship and mission, enabling Christians in a range of professions to make a real difference in an urban world.'

Dr. David Smith, Lecturer in Urban Mission and World Christianity, International Christian College, Glasgow

'a useful and much-needed book'

Richard Tiplady, independent organizational development consultant for missions agencies

The Heavenly Good of Earthly Work

Darrell Cosden

First published jointly in 2006 in the United Kingdom by Paternoster Press and in the United States by Hendrickson Publishers, Inc.
P.O. Box 3473, Peabody, Massachusetts 01961-3473.
Website: www.hendrickson.com

12 11 10 09 08 07 06 7 6 5 4 3 2 1

Paternoster Press is an imprint of Authentic Media
9 Holdom Avenue, Bletchley, Milton Keynes, Bucks., MK1 1QR
Website: www.authenticmedia.co.uk/paternoster
Authentic Media is a division of Send The Light Ltd, a company limited by guarantee (registered charity no. 270162)

British Library Cataloguing in Publication Data
A catalogue record for this book is available from the British Library
ISBN 1-84227-417-1
Library of Congress Cataloging-in-Publication Data
ISBN 1-56563-669-4

Cover Design by Scratch the Sky
Print Management by Adare Carwin
Printed in Great Britain by J.H. Haynes & Co. Ltd., Sparkford

Contents

Acknowledgements vii
Foreword ix

Changing Work
The Heavenly Good of Earthly Work? 1
Isn't Work Killing Us? 3
Faith and Work(s): Bridging the Great Divide? 5
A Health Warning 9

Part I
Ground Down: So Why Doesn't Our View of Work Work?

1. Why Can't I Do God's Work Too? 13
Second-class Christians 16
When Your Call is Higher than My Call 22
Spirit Matters More than Matter? 24
Making Points but Missing the Point 28

2. What on Earth Will Your Work Be Doing in Heaven? 31
In the End Does Matter Matter? 31
A Personal Reflection 33
Starting with Heaven? 36
Ending with Earth? 45

Part II
The Heavenly Future of Earthly Work: What Does the Bible Say?

3. Taking Earth to Heaven: The Resurrection 51
Interpreting Jesus' Resurrection 52

Jesus the Prototype 54
Touch My Hands and Feet 55
Quintessentially Adam 60
The Future of Creation, God's and Ours (Romans 8) 68
Transforming Work (Revelation 21 and 22) 72

4. The Original Job Description: God's Apprentices (Genesis 1 – 11) 78
Where Do I Fit in God's Story? 78
A Play about Work: An Interactive Drama (Genesis 1 – 11) 81
The Stage, the Players and the Acts (Genesis 1:1–2:3) 83
From the Beginning: What on Earth Am I Doing? 86
Promising Failures: God's Image Bearers at Work 89
The Curtain Rises: Act 1, Scene 1 91
Finally a Theology that Works 98

Part III
Heavenly Minded *and* Good for the Earth: Work, Spirituality and Mission

5. Justifying our Work: A Spirituality of Work that Works 103
Salvation with Work, not by Work(s) 105
Modern Work: Bringing Hell to Earth? 108
Judgement Needed 111
Faith Beyond Mere Obedience 118
Partnering with God 121

6. Shaping the Things to Come: Mission for the Masses 125
A Theology of Mission for the Rest of Us 129
A New Kind of Missionary 135
Working in the Spirit: Mission that Works 143
Work: Our Heavenly-Minded Mission 146

For Further Reading 149

Acknowledgements

I would like to express my deepest thanks to all who have contributed in one way or another to making this book. To Robin Parry: thank you for your encouragement and for all your hard work, especially during the proposal and early draft stages. And to Tara Smith: thanks for your contributions to the edited text. Without both of you this project would never have become what it is. To the International Christian College (I.C.C.) in Glasgow: thank you for providing me with a study leave from January to March 2005 to allow me the freedom I needed from normal duties to draft most of the chapters. To the staff and Christian community at the Schloss Mittersill Study Center in Austria: thank you for accommodating me and my family during this time and for welcoming us so openly into your lives. We are changed people for having lived and worked with you for these months. Thank you also for providing me with the most beautiful alpine scenery imaginable as a backdrop to stimulate my thinking and writing.

I would also like to offer thanks to all those who allowed me to test my ideas on them. Thanks to my students at I.C.C., for offering from your own working experiences and reflections numerous priceless insights during the modules on the theology of work. Thanks to the members of the I.C.C. Faculty and Post-graduate Research Seminar, for allowing me to present the ideas that have become Chapter 2 and for offering your discerning insights and critiques. Thanks likewise go to the students in the theology of work course (including my wife Kristy) at the Schloss Mittersill Study Center. I appreciate your enthusiastic interaction with the hot-off-the-press draft of this book. Your openness and passionate engagement with the text, as well as your perspectives from a multitude of cultural contexts, blessed me more than you can ever know.

I also want to thank our cell group at the Bishopbriggs Community Church for reading and discussing a few early drafts of the initial chapters. Your input has proven invaluable, and I thank Craig Anderson for allowing me to refer to our conversations within the text itself.

I also want to thank especially my academic colleagues who carefully read most chapters and offered challenge and correction where needed. Thank you for contributing your specialized expertise in the fields of biblical studies, missiology, and Christian spirituality. Here thanks go to Dr. Andrzej Turkanik at Schloss Mittersill and to Dr. Stephen Chester, Dr. David Smith, Dr. Rory Mackenzie and David Miller at I.C.C. Of course, all failings in the text and inaccuracies are entirely my own.

A final word of thanks goes to John Jeacocke. Thanks for your inspiration and constant encouragement. Thanks also for the many hours you spent reading and modifying the text as well as helping me with all the computing issues.

Changing Work?

The Heavenly Good of Earthly Work?

Does your daily work matter much in the grand scheme of things? Do you feel that you can "make a difference" - whatever that might mean - through your work? Are you investing yourself and your energies in something that really counts?

"Yes!" you might respond confidently. Or you might want to say yes but aren't sure if that's true. You might even be quite certain that your work amounts to very little in life's big picture.

Most of us have probably asked questions about the value or meaning of what we do at work. Since we spend so much of our lives working, it makes sense to pause and reflect upon its purpose. It is quite natural to hope that what we invest our lives in counts for something or serves some greater purpose beyond our own survival.

Stepping back to ponder questions like these can be a bit scary, though. For what if, upon reflection, we conclude "no"? And what if we have had little or no choice about what work we do? Or what if we had a choice, but now in hindsight fear that we made a bad one? Is risking the emotional turmoil of a "no" really worth it?

I believe that it is. For, whether or not we *feel* or *believe* that our work counts for much, this book will argue that it in fact does - or at least it can. And knowing that our work does count ultimately, and why that is so, gives meaning and purpose to life.

Yet dare Christians suggest that we can or should find ultimate meaning and purpose in what we *do*? Is this not dangerous for your spiritual health, or even heretical?

Clearly Christians are concerned about what work means for this life - the earthly good of earthly work. But what about the heavenly good of earthly work? Could your work count for anything from the perspective of eternity? Should you even wonder about this?

The pages that follow develop the idea that understanding the implications of our foundational Christian beliefs will help us to see that what we often call "secular work" is ultimately for "heavenly good." Our everyday work (whether paid or unpaid) actually matters and makes a difference - not just in the here and now, but also for eternity. Work, and the *things* that we produce through our work, can be transformed and carried over by God into heaven.

Further, we will see that belief in the heavenly good of earthly work is the only solid theological basis for experiencing a "spiritual" dimension in our work. Although it is becoming more common these days to suggest that work has spiritual value because we can use the workplace as a platform for ministry and mission as traditionally conceived, this book argues differently. This more narrow view of work's spiritual meaning is inadequate, both because of the theology it teaches and because of what it leads to in the Christian life.

From a Christian point of view, all human work (and not just "religious work") has eternal meaning and value. This value includes work's earthly good - its obvious economic, social, personal (even "spiritual") importance in this life - but it goes well beyond all that.

The heavenly good of earthly work refers to the idea that our ordinary work affects and in some ways actually adds to (though it does not cause, determine or bring about) the ultimate shape of eternity - the new creation. When we grasp this eternal aspect of work, we will have begun to experience the fullness of God's intended purpose for us and for our work.

Initially, such suggestions will almost certainly sound like a strange "new teaching." For those of us raised singing choruses like "the things of earth will soon be past, only what's done for the Lord (i.e., "spiritual ministry," not daily work) will last" these concepts may even sound downright unchristian.

What about our salvation by grace alone, our own inadequacies due to sin, and all we know about the nature of heaven and eternity? Does not our Christian understanding, especially following the Reformation, tell us that no human efforts can be of ultimate spiritual value or "good" before God or for eternity? Therefore, if our "religious" works will not last into eternity, then certainly our "secular" work (no matter how seemingly good our motives or helpful our products) will not last either.

While at first glance it might appear that "the heavenly good of earthly work" undermines the gospel of Christ by suggesting a form of "work(s) salvation," nothing could be further from the truth. Rather, what we will see is the opposite: discounting the heavenly good of earthly work actually undermines the good news of the gospel, and several basic Christian beliefs, thereby jeopardizing for most people the possibility of a genuine Christian life.

Rather than being a dangerous bit of theological speculation, these ideas about work actually reinforce and make more meaningful the doctrines of heaven and salvation by grace alone. Demonstrating this coherently and theologically from Scripture is the primary task of this book.

The focus of this book is upon work in the sense of occupational activity. Yet the ideas explored apply to all of our human activity - what we might call an active human life in the realm of the ordinary. I have not specifically applied these ideas to, for example, those who care for the young, the sick or the elderly at home, the unemployed or the retired. Yet accepting "the heavenly good" of earthly activity will transform how all of these people, too, view their lives.

Isn't Work Killing Us?

To argue for the "earthly good of earthly work," let alone the "heavenly good of earthly work," means swimming against the tide of current wisdom. However, beyond the possible theological objections to the idea, some today would say that it is ill-advised, or indeed even foolish, to attempt to promote a positive view of human work and human intervention and manipulation of the world around us. One might reasonably argue that work is necessary for survival, but in today's globalized McWorld economy many experts argue that work has in many areas brought about more harm than good – for the worker and for the wider environment. A positive assessment of work, then, would seem misguided. For work today often leads us to hell, not heaven.

For so many of us in the west, and throughout the world, work is something we do, and often endure, simply to keep life and limb together. Most of us put up with the difficult realities of our daily work because we have to. Some of us have "good jobs" – paid or unpaid work that we would say we by and large enjoy. Some of us in western consumer cultures have work that gives us financial resources well beyond basic survival, so that we can access what we have come to see as the "good life."

Some of us are even fortunate enough to engage in a particular type of work because it is something we like to do, or because we think we can make a difference through it. Yet, even so, we often find that the reality of our work and working life are less than we had hoped for. If our "real work in the real world" is good at all, it is often only so in a very partial sense – as a means to some other limited, albeit good, end. To ask more from our work and to suggest that it might be of both earthly and eternal value would be seen by many as misguided romanticism at best, outrageous at worst. The results of our work seldom seem to last more than a few days, never mind permanently. Even the repetitive nature of what many of us do daily leads us to the resignation that all we accomplish fades into the past and is lost forever. "Meaningless! Meaningless!" says the teacher in Ecclesiastes, and many of us would concur. "What does man gain from all his labor?"

Yet, even beyond "meaninglessness" there is another, arguably more sinister, danger facing us. Most scientists, sociologists, and psychologists are telling us that our working and our works are killing us and our natural environment. Stress-related illness due to over-work is commonplace in western culture. Human production and consumption lie at the heart of most of the problems in the world. The growing global ecological crisis, the wealth discrepancy between north and south and the instability that this causes, and the countless other global conflicts we face, it is undeniable that our "work" – what we do and how we do it - is to a large extent to blame. If we further consider the social problems like unemployment, underemployment, misemployment, and the growing lack of permanent work in many societies we can understand why Pope John Paul II has argued "that human work is a key, probably the essential key" to most of the social questions we face.[1]

Is it not then naive and even dangerous to suggest to people that their work is good? Dare we go further and suggest that our work can be eternally good?

These realities, as well as the theological questions alluded to above, pose important challenges to the Christian vision that this book presents, and they cannot be glossed over. In order to ground our theology in these real problems of real life, our discussion will seek reasonable answers to such criticisms.

Faith and Work(s): Bridging the Great Divide?

It's clear that, no matter how good it might seem from time to time, work presents many problems for most of us. Sometimes there is no work available at all. At other times there is so much that work dominates and takes over our lives, leaving little time and space for anything else - our families, ourselves, or even

---

1 *Laborem Exercens: Encyclical Letter of the Supreme Pontiff John Paul II on Human Work* (London: Catholic Truth Society, 1981), 3.

"church" activities. Such work-related stress often lies at the heart of our disintegrated lives.

It could be said that work-related questions are actually the main spiritual challenges facing us. Although Christians are beginning to recognize that the church needs to focus on these issues surrounding our work to fulfill her mission, we as churches and leaders often find ourselves ill-equipped to help people deal with and grow within these realities in a spiritually meaningful way. In fact, as we will see in Part I, our theology often inadvertently contributes to the problems rather than providing a genuine way through them. As we will see, this frequently results from under-exploring, misunderstanding, or at least misapplying, some key Christian truths. That is, the way in which we often tell our salvation story leads to a negative view of work and thus to spiritual frustration.

Many churches and church leaders feel frustrated and disempowered in the face of a rapidly changing world where conventional Christian beliefs and practices are increasingly seen to be irrelevant. Rather than cast blame on churches and their leaders, Part I examines the belief structures that often hinder us – thereby clearing the ground for a new way of seeing things. Without this ground-clearing we will be unable to redress the problems that are often by-products of the way we have been taught our beliefs and learned, or not learned, as the case may be, to put them together to address real-world situations.

It is often not clear to many leaders, let alone to ordinary church members, how our Christian beliefs in creation and redemption, resurrection and heaven could relate *directly* to such real-world issues as our work. This is because most of us do not understand why or how we came to formulate our biblical beliefs into specific doctrines. We often don't realize that, throughout history, our brothers and sisters were retelling our common and unchanging story in a particular way and with specific emphases in order to confront the unique problems that they faced. Once we understand that all doctrines are formulated in particular times, places, and situations, we can learn from the successes and failures of those who have gone before us. The benefit of this hindsight will give us insight into how to apply our faith to contemporary problems.

Because the church frequently lacks this theological understanding and leadership training, those who want to dive in and address work-related issues often look for help and resources elsewhere. They conclude prematurely that the answers must lie outside of our Christian beliefs – in, for example, the social sciences, the corporate world, or even non-Christian spiritualities.

This, however, does not need to be the case. While we must learn what we can from other disciplines, Christians have a number of unique resources within the faith itself. Our theology, for example, can address head-on the work-related problems we face. As we explore how the Christian faith provides the resources we need here, we will also find spiritual formation and mission becoming integrated and genuinely a part of our lives rather than supplementary "religious" activities and concerns. An integrated and whole life, including work, is possible. To address the problems associated with our work we need to be able to ask hard questions of our faith and understand how it relates to work. We need a theology and spirituality of work.

Parts 2 and 3 of this book undertake this constructive task. They explore several of the resources God has provided for this purpose - through himself and through the rich heritage of our faith which is our theology. In Part II, "The Heavenly Future of Earthly Work," we start in Chapter 3 by examining how the resurrection of Christ, our resurrection hope, safeguards the value and meaning of our whole lives, including our work. This leads to an exploration of the nature of heaven, or more particularly "the new heavens and new earth" as pictured in Revelation 21 and 22. Chapter 3 considers the ultimate nature and shape of eternity – and the place of human work therein.

Chapter 4 reflects on the foundations of this theology by exploring the early chapters of Genesis. There we mull over what it means to be human and where our work fits into our identity and into God's purposes for us.

What becomes clear in these two chapters is how our everyday work, that in which we invest so much of our lives, can be good and meaningful in relation to both this life and the one to come. Together these chapters show us how our work's ordinary "life" and "spiritual" value are integrated, rather than being distinct or competing forces.

What does it mean to be "Heavenly Minded *and* Good for the Earth"? Part III answers this question by exploring, with an eye to work, the implications for Christian spirituality and mission of the biblical material formulated in Part II.

Chapter 5 develops several key dimensions of Christian spirituality to propose a spirituality of work that will liberate rather than frustrate us. What does it mean to be justified together with our "work(s)" rather than by them? What does it mean to be co-workers with God, given that all our work(s) are subject to the penetrating fires of judgement? A Christian spirituality of work embraces notions of obedience, but it in fact takes us much deeper with God than traditional "obedience-based" Christian spiritualities ever could.

Finally, Chapter 6 explores how this new understanding of work transforms our view of what it means to be involved in missions and to be a missionary. The heavenly and earthly good of our work can be assimilated into a single, purposeful life with a kind of missionary manifesto which is the title of the final chapter – "Shaping the Things to Come: Mission for the Masses."

Chapter 6 offers a way forward for the whole people of God rather than a choice few. As new realities in our work and working life threaten to make the way we experience church irrelevant to most people, this theology of mission provides Christian laypersons and leaders alike with hope and a breath of fresh air.

A Health Warning

A word of warning is in order here, however. Seeing our work differently will not necessarily mean that our work will overflow with meaning and purpose. Such a conviction will gradually transform our inner disposition - our attitudes, motivations, and perspectives. Yet although these are positive changes, they are not what true spirituality is all about.

When we see our work in a new "spiritual" light it becomes more important (not less) to try to change our work's structures and activities. Having a new attitude in an unjust or bad situation is the starting point - not the ending. God calls us to be agents for cultural change and not to be "spiritually" talked into accepting a situation as OK, or even as "God-given," when it is not. The spiritual life requires far more than new beliefs and a new attitude.

New beliefs do, however, stimulate our imaginations and allow us to develop fresh perspectives on our current situations. A new belief about work will enable us, in the Spirit, to interpret and evaluate our work and ways of working in fresh ways so that our "sanctified imaginations" can bring forth seeds of change. We will find ourselves envisioning new work and godly ways of doing our work. From this, and to the degree that we have influence where we work, change will begin to take place. Our spirituality will become real to us and we will begin to flourish as God's people.

PART I

Ground Down

So Why Doesn't Our View of Work Work?

1

Why Can't I Do God's Work Too?

So I hated life, because the work that is done under the sun was grievous to me. All of it is meaningless, a chasing after the wind. I hated all the things I had toiled for under the sun, because I must leave them to the one who comes after me. And who knows whether he will be a wise man or a fool? . . . What does a man get for all the toil and anxious striving with which he labors under the sun? All his days his work is pain and grief; even at night his mind does not rest. This too is meaningless. *Ecclesiastes 2:17–19, 22–23*

Dissatisfaction with the day-to-day reality of our work is an increasingly common phenomenon in societies influenced by western values and ways of doing things. Longer working hours and higher performance expectations have led to a stressed-out workforce.[2] Depersonalization, allowing little room for self-expression and personal development; under-use of our skills and abilities; the pressure to cheat or cut corners – these are just a few of the negative realities that cause many of us to question

[2] According to the Self-reported Work-related Illness (SWI) report published by the Health and Safety Executive, over half a million people in Britain believed that in 2003-04 they were experiencing work-related stress at a level that was making them ill. The Stress and Health at Work Study (SHAW) indicated that nearly 1 in 5 of all working individuals thought their job was very or extremely stressful. According to the National Institute for Occupational Safety and Health website (NIOSH), various surveys indicate that 40 per cent of Americans believe their job "is

whether our work is really worth the investment of so much of our lives.

Of course, worker frustration is not new. It is an experience common to all – even Christians. It is bound up with the fallen human condition. Yet the frustration with work that we will reflect upon in this chapter is different from this shared human reality. Christians sometimes experience a further, distinctively religious, dimension of frustration – something that unfortunately we bring upon ourselves. My experiences teaching on work, both in academic and in various workshop and congregational settings, suggest that a growing number of Christians are what can only be called "spiritually" frustrated in and by their work.

The common effects of our fallenness are, of course, spiritual. But I'm referring to another, often crushing, kind of frustration that many of us feel. This frustration emerges, in fact, from our theology – from beliefs, especially about salvation, that we assume are correct. Many of us in the western church, however, hesitate to question our beliefs about salvation – beliefs we have fought so hard to preserve in the face of opposition. While something doesn't seem quite right to many of us, we reason that our fundamental beliefs can't be wrong. But, unfortunately, these beliefs as we commonly formulate them are the ones that lead us to assign less significance to the work done by those with "ordinary" (as opposed to "ministry") jobs – and herein lies our deepest frustration.

Of course, we might see what we call ordinary work as respectable and even necessary as a discipline so that we can grow spiritually. We might even believe that faithfulness in our work now will lead to some kind of reward in eternity. Some of us might even view work as important strategically, as a platform

---

extremely stressful" (Northwest National Life Survey), 26 per cent say they are "often or very often burned out or stressed by their work" (Families and Work Institute), and 29% of workers say they are "quite a bit or extremely stressed at work" (Yale University).

for evangelism, or primarily as an opportunity to engage in some other ministry – for example, one that allows our real focus to be upon what we think of as a co-worker's "spiritual" state.

Yet many of us nevertheless experience a real spiritual struggle. In spite of all these positives, we wonder whether our work itself really matters – or simply the other things it provides or makes possible. Is there any real lasting or "eternal" value in our work? Most in evangelical circles would concede that in the final analysis – from the perspective of eternity – only things that relate to the soul or a person's inner spiritual state really matter for eternity. At best, ordinary work is seen as a means to these "religious" ends.

I recently had a conversation with a friend on this very topic. Craig is a civil engineer who spends his days designing roads and parking lots. He admitted that he finds it hard to imagine how civil engineering could have any value from the perspective of eternity. (Although he very much wanted to think that it could.) My suggestion that civil engineering could indeed have eternal value excited Craig. He truly enjoys many of the technical aspects of engineering and feels that his work dovetails with, although it does not totally encompass, who God has made him to be.

However, Craig also admitted that when he stands back and thinks about what he does every day, he often feels frustrated. He feels he is failing to make a contribution in really important *spiritual* matters. He wishes that he could do more obviously spiritual ministry than his work allows.

He also sees two advantages to his salary: first, he earns money he can give to various ministries; and, second, his day-job financially supports him to the degree that he can volunteer in the evenings and on weekends for the more fulfilling and "important" ministries at his church. Beyond these things, however, Craig is hard-pressed to see any eternal value in civil engineering.

As we will see in this chapter, thinking like this is actually ingrained in our western Christian spirituality. And it surfaces in our attitudes, practices, and beliefs. But as we recognize the shape that ideas like these frequently take in our language and beliefs we will see more clearly not just why so many Christians have become spiritually frustrated, but also how we might be able to untangle and re-form our beliefs. Although it is necessary to start by deconstructing existing beliefs and attitudes, the goal is a constructive one – to bring into focus a way forward.

For those, however, whose experience in the faith is different, who do not feel the spiritual frustration I am exploring, let this exercise illustrate how beliefs and practices common in many of our churches can inadvertently cause problems.

But many of us have experienced something like this spiritual frustration, and the questions we need to ask are: Where did it come from? Why does our common Christian view of work not work?

Second-class Christians

Who really is doing God's work in their work? This is another way to ask the theological question we are exploring. When asked, a lot of Christians who are engaged in what I am calling ordinary work often tie themselves up in knots. They know that the answer should be that as Christians we all are doing God's work, but they seldom are able to say this is true of themselves – at least not when they think about their work alongside their pastor's or their friends' who are in mission. Usually people avoid answering this question by talking instead about the work that they do outside their occupations in church-based ministries.

While these believers might not be conscious of what they are doing or might be unable to put their feelings into words, clearly anxiety and frustration often lie just below the surface. A little probing will usually bring this out. This is a real spiritual dilemma.

Most of us would like to believe that we are in our particular work and at our specific place of work because God in his providence has, directly or indirectly, led us there. This is one prominent strand of our piety. Whether we view this as a specific calling or simply as where God has us for now, we rightly want to think that, by being where we are, we are accepting the providential workings of God and are therefore living obediently – or at least not disobediently. If we believed that we were out of God's will either morally or specifically we would, if it were possible, seek a change.

If we accept in obedience that we are where God has us for now, we of course should not feel spiritual frustration about this. We know that we can honor and glorify God where he has placed us. We believe that in our work we can love God and, hopefully, our neighbor as well. As the great Reformer Martin Luther taught, this is spiritually speaking our proper place in this life and a proper view of work. Spiritually, at least in this area of our lives, we should be at peace.

However, such peace often proves elusive because another strand of our piety, one particularly central in evangelicalism, unfortunately pushes us in the opposite direction. And here is where the tension develops that many of us feel. This aspect of our piety focuses on the ultimate question of our salvation. It is concerned primarily with evaluating everything we do in this life in relationship to eternity.

This strand of our piety begins with the obvious theological conclusion that if eternity or heaven is ultimate, then what is ultimately important are only the things directly related to it. This is quite a reasonable conclusion. However, it is when we think about our daily work in this way that things get complicated and many of us start to feel like second-class Christians.

We can see this demonstrated in the way many evangelicals understand God's call for some people to enter Christian ministry and make this their work. It starts like this: God calls some from among us into "full-time" or vocational Christian ministry of some sort. Of course we know that such language is awkward since all Christians are called to be full-time servants of God. Therefore, we reason that the special nature of this calling is simply one of function, meaning service, rather than one of status. In itself this is all quite orthodox. God does lead some of us into ministry as our main, even paid, work.

Yet this piety does not leave us here – it has a power and force of its own once it is voiced. People typically think that God *frees up* a few believers to focus their energies on the ministry more directly than others who have a different, more general, calling. That is, other believers recognize them as gifted in special ways and, unlike the rest of us, set apart by God himself for work that will concentrate on spiritual matters pertaining to people's eternal destinies.

Some might overtly refer to this as a "higher calling." Others would find this language offensive. Yet in practice there is little difference. Those with this special call work on the things that really matter. Others do not.

It is hard to imagine how we might conclude differently. The desire for our life's work to be an investment in something we believe to be lasting, even ultimate, is rooted deeply in our spirituality. That is why this idea of "special calling" appeals to many of us. We almost always hear about this kind of "calling" when "ministers" and those training for full-time ministry tell their stories and talk about their work.

Of course, those who embrace this spirituality that necessitates belief in a "special call" don't intend to leave others out, to make some feel they are serving God less because they have a more earthly calling. To avoid such implications, therefore, we often call upon the other strand of our piety – as we proclaim that we all glorify God by being where he has put us.

Yet something does not quite work if we think about what we are saying. When we put these two strands of piety together we are forced to conclude something very strange indeed: God has called a chosen few to serve by focusing on eternal, lasting matters, while he has called others to serve by focusing on earthly, less ultimately important, matters.

If this is true, then some of us are bound to feel frustrated or even hurt – whether we try theologically to soften the blow or not. The logic is relentless. If God has placed some of us in work that does not ultimately make that much difference, we who don't focus full-time on eternal matters are bound to feel the sting.

In practice we can see the dangers of this in more traditional or clerical expressions of the faith. Clericalism, or the belief that those in vocational ministry have a higher status or spiritual value, is a foundational assumption in many churches. The priest, many believe, spends more time in his or her work dealing with the things of eternity – the care of souls and the ministry of the word and sacrament – than do ordinary working Christians in the marketplace or home. A spiritually frustrating hierarchy within the people of God ensues.

Such hierarchical distinctions between the clergy and laity are also in evidence in low-church traditions – among those claiming most fervently to believe in and practice the spiritual priesthood of all believers.[3] The hierarchy in these traditions, however, usually takes the more subtle form of a sacred/secular divide. It is not Christian people, but rather it is work itself that is classified. Work is either sacred or secular – determined by a job's perceived relationship to eternal things.

Traditions influenced by revivalist and pietistic branches of Christianity express this tendency to the sacred/secular divide with some sort of challenge from a preacher, song, or prayer. Each and every true disciple is urged to invest most of his or her life's energy on eternal things rather than working at earthly things that do not last. Although a person's work might be good, "going into the ministry," or at least doing spiritual ministry with the first-fruits of our energies – especially while at work – is better.

What clearly emerges then, whether we want it to or not, is a two-tiered understanding of the Christian life in service to

---

[3] For more detailed discussion of this see R. Paul Stevens, *The Abolition of the Laity: Vocation, Work and Ministry in Biblical Perspective* (Carlisle: Paternoster, 1999).

God. There is a first-class spirituality and special "Lord's work" and therefore, by definition, also a second-class Christianity focused on the things of earth and lived out in ordinary work. The latter is still *sort of* the Lord's work, but it is temporal and thus less meaningful than the former. Both are good, but one is clearly better. I have heard many sermons on Mary and Martha that actively promote this kind of spiritual thinking. Mary, by putting mundane working activities aside and focusing directly on her relationship with Jesus, becomes the spiritual model. She has clearly chosen the best and is more praiseworthy than Martha because she focused on that which will last. Martha, on the other hand, was obsessed with her daily work – and thus on things that are passing away and ultimately less important.

We do not have to look far to find this piety lived out in practice. At a recent graduation ceremony at an evangelical theological college, the speaker passionately challenged the graduates to resist the temptation to leave "the ministry" and undertake other kinds of ultimately less important work when vocational ministry becomes difficult, since this will not count as much for eternity. After the service, a graduate returning to a teaching career in a high school approached me and sarcastically commented about his "already having opted for second best." What else could he conclude?

Subtle and overt expressions of this piety are the norm in many of our churches. We have noted where some of our song lyrics lead us. "The things of earth will soon be past, only what's done for the Lord will last" (since we know it's people that last for eternity, this implies evangelism or the nurture of souls). Then there is the chorus: "Turn your eyes upon Jesus, look full in his wonderful face, and the things of earth will grow strangely dim in the light of his glory and grace."

These songs pick up on common dualities in biblical language, like our earthly/spiritual bodies as well as the spirit/flesh distinctions that Paul makes. However, the songs do not simply allude to these dualities – they also interpret them. And herein lies the question: Does Scripture really teach the kind of duality we often assume it does?

We will explore this question more fully. What is important to note here is that we are conveying, by the songs we sing and even by how we quote Scripture, that some work counts for more because it touches more directly upon eternal matters. This work is a first-rank or first-order Christian activity, as opposed to all other work, which is honorable but is at best second-class because it deals primarily with earthly things.

So what is the average Christian, who spends the vast majority of his or her energies in ordinary work, to conclude from all this? It would seem in practice that the very best most of us could ever hope to be is *second-class* Christians.

This conclusion is bound to cause frustration. Although our hearts may tell us that we *are* doing something spiritually worthwhile since we are obediently doing the ordinary work God has us doing, we will be more persuaded by the other message from our hearts – that time not spent working in evangelism or other "spiritual activities" is actually wasted.

So regardless of our "calling," we face a spiritual dilemma. Most of us only get to spend a small percentage of time devoting our gifts and energies to so-called "eternal things." It appears that we are called to serve God, and serve him in our ordinary work, but that somehow we also need to accept that, unlike the work of full-time ministers, what we do does not ultimately have eternal or lasting value. It's no wonder many Christians are feeling torn and even frustrated in their work.

This tension is often further compounded by the fact that many of us in the west today are constantly being bombarded either with choices about job or career changes, or with the need to make such changes given economic realities. It is increasingly assumed that, for one reason or another, a person will change his or her career at least once. This reality brings opportunity, but also pressure to climb the perceived ladder of spiritual success.

Many Christians, either because they want to grow spiritually or because they feel they already have, feel pressure at times of career change to switch to some form of specifically Christian work. Given a choice, they would rather invest their lives in something more "spiritual."

Yet what if they do not hear God "call" them to do this? Or what if they cannot make this change, for any number of reasons? Then they must simply conclude either that their circumstances are their fault so God can't work through them or that God does not want to use them in the really important things, at least not right now. The conclusion, whether they articulate it consciously or not, is that they really are second-tier, or second-class, Christians.

When Your Call is Higher than My Call

"Second-class" Christians, then, are categorized according to the unofficial "hierarchy of callings" that often emerges in congregational life. This spiritually disastrous practice categorizes people's work in a descending order of value according to perceived spiritual significance. As we have seen, Christians commonly view vocational ministry as a higher calling. But our assumptions about work cause us to make even further distinctions. Subtly, we prioritize even these special callings. A pastor, missionary, evangelist and full-time worker in a Christian agency might all have special ministry callings. But in some circles the missionary or evangelist is seen as having a higher calling than, say, a pastor, because (as ridiculous as this seems) the former appears to focus more, and more directly, upon eternal matters.

In contrast, the second-tier vocations or occupations focus on more mundane realities. As we have seen, if these "earthly vocations" impress upon eternity at all, they are thought to do so only indirectly. And we prioritize these second-level vocations as well. Firstly, we do so according to their perceived earthly good. So the helping professions rank at the top, while the more "selfish" occupations like lawyer, politician, and businessperson are at the bottom.

It is never, of course, this simple in practice. Those at the bottom of this second tier, those perceived to be most tainted by money and power, are often the ones who have skills transferable to lay church leadership positions. Those following these careers are also the ones with more financial resources to give to the church. So, almost paradoxically, these people climb their way back up the ladder of spiritual perception – not because of their work, but because of how they use the fruits of it.

Likewise, those in other middle-of-the-road callings achieve higher spiritual status if they are seen to spend enough time attending church meetings or serving in the church. To complicate matters, people in the helping professions often end up ranking even lower on this scale because their demanding work generally allows less time and money to devote to church life.

As cynical as my musings here may sound, they only slightly overstate the reality in many congregations. Anyone attempting to navigate the corridors of this spirituality or hierarchy of calling will soon find that it is a complicated business. It is, of course, implicit and not always conscious. This perception of hierarchy only serves to contribute further to an underlying spiritual frustration among many ordinary working Christians.

This hierarchy of callings is rooted deeper in our spirituality than we might imagine, however. It does not simply result from our human inconsistencies or frailties in applying otherwise "sound" theological truth. Problematical hierarchies are at the heart of how we in the west commonly understand the Christian story.

A hierarchy of callings emerges naturally enough because, deep down, many of us believe that God designed creation itself to be hierarchical.[4] It is not just that hierarchical thinking

[4] If we believe that God himself represents some kind of hierarchy in God's internal Trinitarian relationships, and that people called to image him should do likewise in their social lives, then it is only

is deeply engrained in our practices; it is also woven into the very structures of our beliefs. To understand this we need to recognize that, in its most basic form, a spirit-material dualism (or hierarchy) has in fact been a building block in western thinking for most of the last two millennia – and in western theology, both Catholic and Protestant, we can see this clearly.

Throughout the rest of this chapter and the next one we will examine how and where such dualistic beliefs and assumptions have played a role in the structuring of our beliefs. We begin with an example from Roman Catholic thought that, in the process of teaching many important things about ordinary work, illustrates what western Christianity, both Catholic and Protestant, has by and large believed – that God has created in the very fabric of reality a hierarchy in which the spiritual realm is higher in rank than the material.

In Chapter 2, in the process of thinking more carefully about whether our work really does need to survive and shape eternity to be "ultimately" valuable, we will explore Martin Luther's theology – the superstructure for so much of Protestant theology and the basis of the tradition of pietism and, eventually, evangelical piety. There we will find a distinctively Protestant form of this dualism.

Spirit Matters More than Matter?

In order to better grasp the shape and impact of that Protestant spirit-material dualism, however, we will first consider the western Catholic tradition out of which it grew and to which it reacted. This tradition is no more succinctly summarized than in the 1981 tract by John Paul II entitled *Laborem Exercens* ("On

---

natural that the cosmos will likewise reflect an ordering consistent with God's own being. For an evaluation of whether God himself exhibits some sort of hierarchy see Jürgen Moltmann, *The Trinity and the Kingdom of God: The Doctrine of God* (London: SCM; San Francisco: Harper & Row, 1981).

Human Work"). In fact, this short pamphlet sums up what most western Christians, even evangelicals, claim to believe about God's ordered design of the cosmos, if not about work itself.[5]

Laborem Exercens is one of a series of pastoral letters, called encyclicals, written occasionally by successive popes since 1891 to be circulated throughout the church. Like the other encyclicals, this one seeks to guide the church in addressing pressing cultural issues. Pastoral in style, *Laborem Exercens* is actually a personal reflection from John Paul II that builds upon the church's theological heritage to offer the outline for a spirituality and ethics of work for late- and post-industrial societies.

Laborem Exercens presents a Christian alternative to the modern economist or materialist view of work that threatens to destroy people and the environment. It reasons from the scriptural account in Genesis that work can and should be both for our benefit and for the benefit of creation as a whole. It shows, biblically and theologically, the value of work and its place in this life that includes, but also goes beyond, the production of material wealth. It outlines how our work helps us to explore, discover and express our humanity to reflect God's image.

In doing this the encyclical demonstrates clearly the importance of work for building society, meaning the family and the broader community, and it shows how through this work God works so that people can flourish. It likewise makes clear the positive place of the church – both to co-operate with God in the world through ordinary work and to equip members of the body for a Christian life and ministry at work. In sum, it shows us the importance and meaning of earthly work.

Yet how this letter goes about doing this is as telling for our purposes as what it proposes. Pope John Paul II's overarching concern in this tract is to make clear that the church has always

---

[5] For a more detailed evaluation of *Laborem Exercens*, see my book *A Theology of Work: Work and the New Creation* (Paternoster Theological Monograph Series; Carlisle: Paternoster Press, 2004), 24–35.

believed that "in the first place work is 'for man' and not man 'for work' " (*LE*, 6). In itself, this statement does not seem particularly controversial. In fact, it appears to echo Jesus' statement in Mark 2:27 that the Sabbath was made for man and not man for the Sabbath. Yet a deeper look at what Pope John Paul II means begins to reveal a dualistic and hierarchical understanding of things.

To substantiate his conclusion, John Paul II outlines two senses of work in *Laborem Exercens*. The first is what he calls the "objective sense" of work, which focuses on the goal of work that is external to the working person – work's material nature and products, understood primarily in economic or material terms. For Pope John Paul II, this is unquestionably one important aspect of work.

The "subjective sense" of work, however, is the one that Pope John Paul II believes to be more important spiritually. The subjective sense focuses on the working person rather than on either the work itself or the use of its products by others. The concern here is with how our work impacts us as persons existentially, socially and spiritually.

John Paul II makes this distinction between work's objective and subjective senses because, as he sees it from a Christian point of view, western society has lost its way by only recognizing the objective sense. As a result, we have become materialist.

Accordingly, we have erred in one of two ways. We have either valued the material over the personal/spiritual or we have placed both on the same level. In the modern west, as John Paul II rightly discerns, we have mostly ordered the objective sense of work over the subjective. Furthermore, but with no less dangerous consequences as he sees it, some have tried to correct this error by doing away with a "right hierarchical ordering" altogether and valuing both subjective and objective aspects of work on the same level. From his theological viewpoint, this approach equally strays from God's design.

The argument he puts forth boils down to the conclusion that, theologically, a hierarchical ordering of the subjective sense of work over the objective should always be maintained – because this accurately reflects God's pattern for ordering the world. In political and economic terms, the priority from a theological point of view should always be labor over capital. In human terms, we must maintain the primacy of persons over things. In the spiritual realm, the priority is always the spiritual over the material – or, as John Paul II says in a related encyclical, we believe in "the superiority of spirit over matter."[6]

The priority of persons over things for western Christians, Roman Catholic and Protestant, is almost beyond question. Whether we see this only in earthly terms for the sake of ethics, or in eternal/spiritual terms relating to a person's eternal destiny, western Christianity traditionally holds this to be a basic Christian belief.

The implications of this idea for spirit-matter dualisms in general and a hierarchy of callings in particular, however, could not be clearer. Ordinary work, what we in the Protestant tradition often refer to as "secular calling," primarily deals with the physical or material, earthly side of reality. Spiritual calling, or what our tradition often refers to as "sacred" work, primarily deals with spiritual, personal, or eternal/heavenly matters. If we hold, as John Paul II does, to the strict priority of the spiritual – persons over the material – then work that deals primarily with the spiritual is bound to be somehow superior to that which deals primarily or only with earthly, material reality. Spiritual callings are bound to be thought of as higher callings. We are bound to rank our work according to its perceived relationship to spiritual reality. A hierarchy of callings is a built-in by-product of the theological belief in the absolute priority of persons over things.

---

[6] Pope John Paul II, *Redemptor Hominis: An Encyclical Letter* (London: Catholic Truth Society, 1979), 16.

Making Points but Missing the Point

It would be wrong to dismiss either *Laborem Exercens* itself or the broader ideas it offers as unhelpful to our theological thinking about work. Indeed the opposite is the case. Although we will further explore the biblical, theological, and practical problems with this view that God has instituted and operates a "spirit over matter" dualism, using this document to highlight these deeper theological questions is only one part of the story. *Laborem Exercens* does make some very important points about work that should not be overlooked.

Although the results of a hierarchy that strictly orders persons over things and spirit over matter are harmful, it is nevertheless essential to critique and challenge the dominant materialism that both destroys personhood and displaces eternal matters. On this latter point, this document speaks an important prophetic word. In rejecting the hierarchy we must be careful not to end up with mirror opposite side effects that lead to, or reinforce, the materialism that is even more devastating than the spiritual problem we are trying to solve.

What *Laborem Exercens* offers is a genuine theological alternative to the mainstream materialistic view of life and work found in the beliefs and values of western modernity. *Laborem Exercens*, and other expressions of piety that offer parallel visions, can do the church a great service. They make valid points but miss the central point, failing as they do to adequately address the spiritual frustration that grows out of a hierarchy of callings.

Although John Paul II states that our work in itself has positive value, not just for life in this world but also from the perspective of eternity, I doubt that the theological basis of his argument can solve the problems grounded in such hierarchical assumptions.

He suggests that our work is somehow gathered up into Christ's suffering and toil in his work on the cross. This idea provides stimulating food for thought. It is appealing to think that, in a real way, our work is taken into Christ's, and that human work becomes a participation in and reflection of Christ's work (not a contribution to it) which could be called a co-working and co-suffering with Christ for our ultimate sanctification. This understanding of work does suggest that work has value in relationship to eternity because it mirrors, and thus points to, eternal/spiritual things.

With this account, Christ's overcoming in the resurrection then becomes the basis for his exaltation to authority over creation. He is the new creation. We too, John Paul II suggests, as we live our resurrected life now, announce the values of the new heaven and new earth in our work.

Whether or not we would find the connections between Christ in his work on the cross and our own work theologically convincing, we are still left with larger questions. Is it our work itself that has value in and for eternity, or is its eternal value found only in what our working does to our souls? The answer, according to John Paul II, seems to be the latter. Further, is work's specifically new creation value according to John Paul II that the work itself will last, like people and their souls? Or is work spiritually valuable only as a pointer toward the new creation through its ethical out-workings in this current life? The answer for John Paul II seems to be that the material aspects of work (its objective sense) will not themselves last. Its value in relation to eternity is solely as a witness to it – work anticipates the new creation concretely in this life. While these are fruitful questions to consider, the basic assumptions underlying *Laborem Exercens* are such that a hierarchy of callings, and the resulting worker frustration, continue to lurk and threaten to torment the saints.

We must now consider whether or not the question as we are posing it is theologically legitimate. Does our work (and in some way its products) need to be "saved" by God to be meaningful or valuable in the final analysis? Although claiming that this is in fact the case might help us pragmatically in overcoming the spiritual frustration caused by a hierarchy of callings, the more fundamental question is, of course, whether this view is true biblically and theologically. We want a solution, a view of work that works. But if the question is wrong because it assumes wrong beliefs, then the answer, although appearing to satisfy for a while, will eventually also be shown to be a view of work that does not work.

We need, then, to explore whether the idea "not eternal not valuable" is legitimate. Although the real biblical and theological test will come from our reflections on Scripture in Part II, we proceed now to clarify what the idea is and is not saying.

2

What on Earth Will Your Work Be Doing in Heaven?

"I am making everything new!" *Revelation 21:5*

In the End Does Matter Matter?

"The significance of secular work depends upon the value of creation, and the value of creation depends upon its final destiny."[7] So explains the Croatian-born Yale theologian Miroslav Volf. If this belief about the material creation is on target then our work, which is no less a part of the physical creation than humanity itself, necessarily becomes "spiritual" and filled with meaning in an ultimate sense. If Volf is right, then we can talk about the heavenly good of earthly work.

Conversely, if work, which has significantly shaped the current order of this creation, is not understood to be an object of God's final salvation, we would then strictly speaking deny the possibility that it is *in itself* ultimately meaningful. As we will see in this chapter, were we to conclude this, the best that we could say would be that work is of earthly good – meaning that it is significant in the more restricted sense of what it makes possible beyond itself for our temporary earthly existence only. Although this conclusion would still allow for work to be spiritually meaningful to a limited degree, if our work is not, like

[7] Miroslav Volf, *Work in the Spirit* (Oxford: OUP, 1991; repr. Eugene, OR: Wipf & Stock, 2001), 93.

we are, open to the possibility of salvation, then to try to develop the high spirituality of work I am suggesting would be pointless.

So consider the question: What is your *initial* gut-level response to the suggestion that your work has to be "saved" to be truly meaningful? This is significant. For this "intuitive" response will help you bring to the surface what your deeply held beliefs actually are about the value of God's physical creation – including where you see the place of work therein. But equally important, and beyond your initial reaction, is what you finally decide about the future of creation. For the implications of that will be immense for your own theology and spirituality of work.

We have seen the theological presupposition of the priority of persons over things in *Laborem Exercens*, which as applied in that context expressed the belief that ultimately spirit is of a higher order than matter. This meant that work's secondary, or "objective" sense, by virtue of its being based in material existence, must be less significant than its "subjective" sense, which focuses upon the inner spiritual disposition of the worker firstly and then on work's derivative value as a witness to the kingdom. This understanding of the value of the material creation – including, it seems, its future – is different from the understanding that theologians like Volf and myself are proposing.

Fundamentally, the vision in *Laborem Exercens* simply recasts western medieval thinking in contemporary form. Theologians in the Middle Ages did value work as a means to a spiritual end and classed work as either active or contemplative. The "active life" was understood to be one occupied with transient things that would not last eternally. The spiritual and eternal value of the work of the active life was understood at best as being only indirect. It made physical survival possible for all. But, what is arguably more important, this work provided the means to enable those called to the higher "spiritual" life to work on these more eternally worthwhile matters pertaining to heaven. This special calling, the "contemplative life," was necessarily the calling of a relatively small minority.

Yet both of these categories of "call," the active and the contemplative, like *Laborem Exercens* today, beg the most basic question. What is the future of the whole of the material creation? What is it that God will save in the end? Is it simply the inner man/soul, people as a unity of body/soul, or even more?

To be theologically consistent, we as Christians should value most highly whatever God values (as determined by what he will save). Thus, work that is occupied with these things that are important to God will be ultimately significant spiritually and most meaningful.

Most evangelicals are used to thinking about salvation in terms of souls, or the inner *spiritual* self. Fewer of us, even though technically we might believe in it, are used to thinking through the meaning and implications of believing in Christ's, and thus our own, bodily resurrection. Fewer still have contemplated what this more physical understanding of salvation might mean for the material dimensions of our creation, including our work.

Throughout the chapters that follow we will ask these questions related to the lasting value of creation, rigorously putting our assumptions to the test as we explore Scripture. Yet at this stage, before becoming absorbed in the biblical details, we need to further consider the practical implications of our inherited popular and theological views of heaven and what we understand "salvation" will include.

A Personal Reflection

The latter years of the 1970s were formative ones for my social and spiritual development. As young Christian teens my friends and I, like many in our tradition, were obsessed with heaven. Being saved was what really mattered, and seeing others saved was our driving mission. Going to heaven was our first fixation. How soon we were going to get there by means of the rapture was our second.

When I was thirteen, I attended a summer camp where a Bible college professor, teaching on Ezekiel, explained to us that in all probability Jesus would return before the end of 1979 – a year and a half away. Armed with this belief and timescale, I became a practical theologian.

How I should live my life as a result of this belief was self-evident to me. I spent my first year in high school stuffing "turn or burn" tracts into lockers rather than studying. After all, what difference would study make for an eternity that was just around the corner? I would not make it past my second year in high school anyway, so why concern myself with grades? Since people's final destiny was at stake, and since there was not much time left, it was obvious to me where I should invest my energies.

Although you might think such activity foolish, my theological reasoning at that time was really quite sophisticated and consistent. More consistent, it seems to me now, than many who believed like me yet did not live/work as if they did. I had grasped the logic that eternity, our final destiny, is what ultimately matters. With childlike clarity and abandon I simply lived what I believed. It made theological sense. God and people are eternal, everything else is temporary. Invest life's energies in eternal things.

Of course, Jesus did not return by the end of 1979. For me, as you might imagine, this sparked somewhat of a crisis of faith. Besides now needing to begin to study a little, I also began to question whether "heaven" really was the most important thing and whether it should be a Christian's primary motivation.

Over the next several years I met Christians from other traditions who happily showed me a new way. Heaven was still important, so evangelism remained important, but it was not all that there was to the Christian life. According to these Christians, evangelism and a concern for things eternal should be thought of as only a few spokes in the wheel that is the Christian life. God has called us to be faithful in earthly matters, too, and obedience in earthly things was, for most of us, to be our prime motivation. Eternity, earthly life, and yet a few other "spokes" needed to balance the wheel otherwise it would not roll along properly. The hub was not heaven but rather God's glory, which we serve by faithful obedience.

Although evangelism was still quite important, now it was for the sake of obedience to God, and not because of a responsibility to accomplish anything of heavenly value. I needed to remember that ultimately God would take care of people's destinies. My job was simply to be faithful in the ordinary life and in witnessing, living what we then called "a balanced Christian life." What God wants of us in this life is to be faithful where he has us. We work on earthly things because God wants us to. We witness faithfully because he wants us to. Since God is head of all things, all activities find their ordering only in relation to God's lordship. For us, obedience is what counts.

We might want to think of heaven for inner motivation when we need a spiritual boost – remembering that this is our destiny. Yet "heaven ain't all there is" said a Christian pop song at the time. Of course, if we use our work or school as a platform for evangelism (or if while at a secular university we put most of our energies into evangelizing and student ministry) then we will have managed to bring the spiritual aspects of heaven and earth together.

During this time in my spiritual adolescence I left my childish ways and became a spiritual realist. Obsession with heaven, getting there quickly by the rapture, and the way this motivated me to live my life was replaced by something akin to the other strand of piety we saw in Chapter 1. I would serve God by being a good student. Obedience, not heaven, became my central concern and the spiritual center from which I lived. Again, I was a practical theologian at work.

Yet to be honest, even during those years of "spiritual realism" the deep-seated beliefs I held about heaven did not really disappear. It was just that I didn't know where they fitted anymore. Seeing heavenly motivation as simply one distinct dimension within the Christian life didn't seem theologically right. This world is passing away and in the end the only things left are God, heaven, and people. With this view of reality, it is difficult to understand heaven as but one of several important concerns.

Yet going back down the theological cul-de-sac I had been stuck in before was definitely not appealing. Until I began post-graduate study, my way of dealing with my uncertainty about the place of heaven in the Christian life was, quite frankly, to suppress it. Yet deep down in my heart I knew that heaven and eternity should be what really mattered. After all, it is our final destiny.

With both of these strands of evangelical piety somewhat incoherently embedded in my practice, and with one or the other surfacing depending upon the spiritual need of the moment, I continued to train for, and finally entered, pastoral ministry and then cross-cultural mission. I have to admit that, deep down, what motivated me was the desire to invest my life not just in something good, but in what is best. I felt compelled by God and really did want my work to count for eternity in ways that it seemed to me, theologically speaking, the work of others no less committed or obedient to Christ unfortunately would not.

I suppose, therefore, that what I am calling the second strand of my evangelical piety, the priority of eternity, was still at work. Sometimes it lurked below the surface, sometimes above it, sometimes I recognized it, sometimes not. What I could not do at this point in my life, however, was leave behind either strand of piety that had become so much a part of my Christian story and pilgrimage for many years. Both, it seemed to me, were correct biblically – even if practically their incompatibility led me to a kind of spiritual schizophrenia.

Starting with Heaven?

Although this is my story, many of the issues I faced are not unique. Many fellow evangelicals tell me of similar experiences of trying to hold together two spiritualities that in reality are suggesting somewhat different visions of the Christian life. But where do these two strands of piety come from and why have so many of us come to believe that the balanced Christian life should involve holding paradoxical, or even contradictory, spiritualities like these together in tension? Where does this emphasis on eternity, the conviction that what ultimately matters is our final destiny, come from? And where does the belief come from that says we should accept "where we are" in obedience as God's providence and simply live out God's call on our life there, regardless of whether or not it seems to focus directly on the really important things, like people's eternal destiny?

The Bible, of course, clearly teaches us that we should be obedient to God whatever our circumstances (1 Cor. 7:17). It also teaches us that our eternal destiny is ultimately important (Matt. 16:26). Yet to conclude from this that the tension in our piety must simply be a creative biblical paradox is neither necessary nor accurate.

This is because the current emphasis of biblical teachings like these and the way we make sense of them together developed at a critical moment in our Christian history. In order to better understand this and to see how and why we as evangelicals have developed and expressed our piety the way we have, we need to look back to what for evangelicals is the defining moment, the Protestant Reformation.

Of course, obedience in our lot in life and getting to heaven were common Christian concerns in medieval Europe also. The threat of not getting to heaven was used by both the western Church and Christendom's secular powers to keep people spiritually and politically in line. The fear of not getting to heaven also led some to pursue a "called" or religious life in the monasteries. Medieval Catholic piety also produced a hierarchy of callings.

Evangelical piety, however, while concerned with these same issues, came to take a quite different shape than that of the medievals. Our understanding of obedience, our beliefs about heaven and our way of seeing eternal things in relation to earthly things really begins with the great reformer Martin Luther. Although John Calvin and the Calvinist tradition have also contributed to the shape of evangelical piety, it is Luther's way of interpreting the Bible (transmitted to us through Pietism and later Revivalism) and the theological formulae that he creates out of this interpretation that provide the superstructure for the aspects of evangelical piety I have outlined.

Like those of many of us in the Protestant evangelical tradition, Luther's beliefs were by and large shaped by his own personal question: What must I, a sinner drowning in guilt, do to be accepted by God and thus granted eternal life and spiritual freedom from this personal guilt? This was not a new question for a monk to ask. But Martin Luther's spiritual innovation lies in a theological revolution where he "rediscovered" and reformulated the belief that we are accepted by God and thus get into heaven irrespective of our actions – by grace *alone* through faith *alone* because of Christ's finished work on the cross.

Contrary to beliefs common in the Roman Church at that time, as Luther saw it God's basis for forgiving us was not to be understood as faith, a gift received solely from God, working itself out in our lives as a love for God and our neighbor. We are not forgiven because we love God or anyone else. Rather, God forgives and can count us as righteous, and thus as acceptable for heaven, on a different basis altogether.

A central strand in Luther's thinking, and what most Protestants following him have emphasized, is that Christ on the cross replaces us, or takes our place before the Father. There Christ paid our penalty for sin's guilt and innocently suffered instead of us. Since as an innocent he suffered our punishment, God's justice is satisfied. Thus, God can now, and only on this basis, justly justify us.

However, God doesn't do this because he looks at us and sees our efforts to love him or our neighbor. Instead he sees Christ and his perfect work of obedience. Thus, we receive our justification not primarily *in* ourselves but rather as we through faith are united to him – or, to be more precise, through faith experienced in baptism, which is where faith finds a word of promise united to a physical sign. That is, God declares and counts us as if we were wholly righteous, even though we are not, because we are "hidden" in Christ who in fact was wholly righteous. This changes us, but only as we live in him, not in ourselves. Another, more nuanced, way of expressing Luther's view is that through faith the church enters into a marriage with Christ. What is ours (unrighteousness) becomes his, and what is his (righteousness) becomes ours. Faith joins us to Christ, and his righteousness is simply a gift from God. We receive this gift of faith, and thus salvation, by God's grace alone. That is, even faith is not a human work but rather a work of God that he has done for us in Christ.

For Luther all things in life, including so-called religious works and ordinary human work, must be judged and find their "place" first and foremost with reference to salvation, or justification appropriated by faith. This means that ultimately everything – all earthly works and all human activity, whether religious or not – must be judged in the light of their eternal value. Contrary to standard medieval thinking, for Luther human secular work should not firstly be evaluated from the point of view of its worth in the Christian social order, as to whether such a work loves God by sustaining social harmony. A view similar to this finds its place in Luther's thinking, but only after the first, more important, eternal evaluation is made.

So what does Luther's new approach to the Christian life that emerged from this mean, and how does it work in practice? How did it come to shape us?

This way of unpacking the gospel story and this understanding of the way salvation works became for Luther the only starting point for Christian thinking as well as for life as a Christian. It became the basis or presupposition around which all other Christian beliefs had to be reshaped. It was only when reflecting on how the doctrine of justification by faith must reform the whole of theology that Luther came to realize that ethics, Christian life in this world, must be reformed as well.

Our motivation for Christian living must change, since our goals and understanding of what we can accomplish spiritually in this life had changed. In short, our whole way of living – our spirituality and ethics – also needed to change.

Of course this meant from the outset that the hierarchy of callings that had grown up in the context of medieval Christianity was fatally flawed. Luther was incensed by the spiritually dangerous beliefs and practices that he rightly saw cutting the masses off from heaven and from the genuinely spiritual life on earth. As Luther had experienced himself, this was a hierarchy claiming that activities and works of a particularly religious nature, like almsgiving and pilgrimages (the contemplative life), were counted as valuable in our journey toward final salvation. Within the medieval system, the activities of the contemplative life were seen as spiritually more valuable than works of a more mundane nature that only yielded earthly blessings that come from keeping the social order on track. Therefore, those who did these religious works, like monks, were thought to have a higher and thus more spiritual calling than others who focused on mundane material existence.

Contrary to this view, Luther had rediscovered the starting point for the Christian life to be justification by faith alone for everyone (the priesthood of all believers). This obviously undermined the whole system of piety claiming that acceptance by God was *guaranteed* only to the few who could spend their lives "at work" devoted to such eternal matters.

Given the nature of justification, no calling or work could ever be seen as spiritually higher than any other. This is because no work(s) can be spiritually good – that is, of any heavenly good – since no work(s) can contribute anything to us spiritually in our ultimate journey toward eternal salvation.

Thus collapsed the hierarchy of callings Luther faced. The doctrine of justification demolishes the medieval hierarchy of callings because nothing that we do has any positive value in relation to heaven.

But what goes in its place? Where do good works or good work fit in? In order to reshape Christian living and ethics to be consistent with justification, Luther reinterpreted several familiar spiritual concepts, at the heart of which was the biblical notion of God's "calling" to us. The rallying point of Luther's new understanding of calling became 1 Corinthians 7:17, which he translated "remain in the calling (work/station) you were in when you were called (to salvation)."

Contrary to the common assumption, however, Luther was not the first to see a person's ordinary work as part of their calling from God. As we have seen, medieval piety was built around the idea that there were two types of callings from God – the religious and the mundane (or active). The latter sustained the social harmony of Christendom. Staying where God's providence put you in life and accepting this obediently was thus the way medievals understood God's will on earth to be accomplished by most people.

Luther's view is not really that different from this, at least concerning the calling to the active life. His innovation, however, was to see all people, including those called to an earthly vocation, as part of the calling to salvation. Luther extracted the notion of calling from the world of medieval Christendom and creatively recast it within his new theological framework. Most commentators suggest that Luther did this with a somewhat imaginative and, frankly, questionable interpretation of 1 Corinthians 7:17–24. But ultimately the new shape of "calling," and the view of work that grows out of it, owe more to Luther's wider theological logic than to his specific interpretation of this passage.

Luther's understanding of calling (or "vocation" as it is from the Latin), his view of ordinary work within that, and the new ethical framework he builds to incorporate it, is an enormous and complex subject. A remarkable amount of helpful literature is available to explain these ideas. These studies usually discuss Luther's understanding of 1 Corinthians 7:17 – "remain in the calling (work/station) you were in when you were called" with the details and debates surrounding his arguments. They also unpack further Luther's idea that when God calls us to himself for salvation, this includes a call to accept our job, social "stations" or roles in life, or profession as directly coming from him and as our primary way to love our neighbor.[8]

Of course, this is where the one strand of piety we have been thinking about comes from – the one focused on obedience in our earthly calling and on accepting our ordinary work as coming providentially from God. For, in contrast to the medievals, to Luther all callings and work therein are equal.

Yet with this belief Luther was not primarily, as we now often mistakenly imagine, trying to raise our estimation of the spiritual value of ordinary work. That is, he was not suggesting that human work is holy or sacred or that it has any *spiritual* or heavenly value. Precisely the opposite is the case.

For Luther any such suggestion would be a hideous idea, because it would land us right back in the problem of needing to merit our own salvation – only this time with mundane rather than religious works. Rather, with his new understanding of calling Luther was first and foremost trying to safeguard his belief in the utter bankruptcy of any work – especially religious work(s), but not exclusively so – with reference to eternity or salvation. The helpful by-product of his approach was the understanding that now "in faith," and only in faith, the whole of a Christian's life, including his or her work, becomes sacred. But even here, it is not sacred in the sense that it has any eternal or heavenly value – other than possibly indirectly by being our form of participation in the sufferings of Christ, and thus an important part of our spiritual growth.

---

[8] See for further reading: Gustaf Wingren, *The Christian's Calling: Luther on Vocation* (Edinburgh: Oliver & Boyd, 1957); Paul Althaus, *The Ethics of Martin Luther* (Minneapolis: Augsburg Fortress, 1972); and Gary Badcock, *The Way of Life: A Theology of Christian Vocation* (Grand Rapids: Eerdmans, 1998).

Ordinary work is only sacred in a secondary or instrumental sense – in that it is now the appropriate obedient earthly response to God's saving grace and general providence. Work in no way secures or, technically speaking, co-operates with this grace to any heavenly end.

Only in this way, as Luther saw it, can human life and work be freed from compulsiveness and set aside to be itself before God, and thus sacred. This way of thinking is the main point of Luther's 1520 *Treatise on Good Works*.

As Luther teased out these details and the absolute distinction between faith and works, a unique approach to spirituality and ethics began to emerge. What resulted was a framework for piety and ethical living ordered around what he saw as two kingdoms, or two governments.

According to Luther, the Christian lives in two spheres, or governments, under God. These are as opposite from one another as faith is from works and as heaven is from earth, although both do depend upon each other and are essential in God's order.

The spiritual kingdom or government in Luther's view is strictly heavenly. It is Christ's kingdom of the gospel and is focused on the "inner man" receiving eternal life – heavenly life through justification alone. It is the kingdom where the Spirit leads people to faith so that, in faith, Christ's lordship is exercised in a person's *heart*. The cornerstone of the heavenly kingdom is justification – eternal life which is God's final destiny for us and what matters in the final analysis. The spiritual kingdom that focuses on the inner man (spirit) rather than the outer man (material and earthly life) is the ultimate standard by which to order and evaluate all of life, including our work(s) which, spiritually speaking, have no heavenly value.

The earthly kingdom in contrast is not, as one might jump to conclude, worthless in God's sight. Nor, strictly speaking, is it "secular," as if it has nothing to do with God. It is part of the spiritual life. However, it is strictly subordinate to the heavenly kingdom. It is, as the twentieth-century Lutheran pastor and theologian Dietrich Bonhoeffer explained, the penultimate kingdom. The earthly kingdom finds its place, and therefore its value, in its service to the heavenly kingdom – the ultimate. The worldly government, like the heavenly, is instituted and administered by God – but it is concerned with the "outer" rather than the "inner" man. Its purpose is always to point to the inner man and thereby direct us to justification, which consists of a righteousness distinct from us but through which we now live.

The earthly government is concerned with more than politics, however, as the term might suggest. The earthly kingdom includes everything important to this earthly life – everything that is of earthly good. This includes marriage and family as well as business and work. The earthly kingdom necessarily is a part of the God-given "orders of creation." It cannot, however, be a part of the "order of redemption," for this would suggest that the things that we do in this life, our work(s), would in some way be of heavenly good – in which case we would find ourselves back trying to justify ourselves by our work(s).

When it comes to our calling to salvation, or vocation, we need to remember that although this is a one-time event, it has two sides leading in opposite directions. There is the heavenly side leading toward our salvation. But there is also the earthly side pointing toward the earthly kingdom and the orders of creation. And it is here that people live out their providentially determined calling from God in whatever place, role, or "station" they find themselves. In relation to heaven, a person's calling in this sense has as much to contribute as their good works – that is, nothing. Ordinary work exists in this life and for this life only. Our calling in the earthly kingdom is our means to love God and our neighbor, but in response to our salvation rather than as part of our path of transformation toward it.

Our calling, when expressed as work, is simply God's providential way of meeting our own and our neighbor's physical needs. This is similar to the medieval view. Our work, or calling, thus finds its spiritual home in this earthly life only. It has no direct value in the light of eternity. It indirectly serves eternity as the penultimate serves the ultimate, but neither our calling to our station nor our work itself is directly of any heavenly or eternal good.

Luther's genius and the spiritual helpfulness of this new view of faith and life cannot be overestimated. Firstly, and crucially for the argument we are developing in this book, Luther shows us the importance of seeing eternity, the new creation, or heaven as the starting point for reshaping piety. This is a piety for the whole people of God rather than just for a select few with special religious or higher callings. Although we will develop this insight in the pages that follow quite differently than Luther did, a point that we share in common is the view that all of life should be ordered to, and take its direction from, our eternal destiny which is heaven.

Secondly, Luther's genius also lay in his extracting the doctrine of vocation from the complex theological system undergirding medieval Christendom that suggested that we needed to acquire merit for salvation through our work(s). Work(s) released from this burden and lived out of the freedom of our salvation make possible an approach to work that will work. At the very least, Luther has made it possible for ordinary believers to readily grasp both salvation and also a spiritual life in and through an ordinary working existence. In this, Luther has a lot to teach us.

Ending with Earth?

Luther's progress, however, comes with a hidden spiritual cost – a cost that Luther himself would not have foreseen. A lot has been made over the years of the suggestion that Luther's two kingdom theology inadvertently provided a base on which the Nazis could build their ideology and co-opt the church. This criticism of Lutheran ethics was behind Karl Barth's now famous "NO" in his debate with the Lutheran theologian Emil Brunner. This, however, is not the cost to which I refer.

The predicament before us now relates to the way Luther's theology of calling and the two kingdoms has influenced how many of us as evangelicals today theologically understand our ordinary work before God. The cost inherent in this does not result necessarily from Luther's insistence on justification as the starting point of the Christian life. In this he was quite right. Rather, the problem lies with the way he limited the value of work to this earth – which stems from his using justification as the hub around which to build his doctrine of vocation and approach to ethics. For although Luther overcame the medieval Christian hierarchy of callings and its spiritually debilitating depreciation of mundane work (the active life), Luther inadvertently also put in its place a new hierarchy of callings that lands us right back in the same spiritual dilemma regarding our ordinary work.

How so? As we have seen, Luther's theology cut off the possibility that the religious or mundane work of ordinary believers might be of heavenly value. Our ordinary work, the only "valuable" work there is in his view, is only ever of earthly value – spiritual earthly value of course, but of no eternal value. Obviously this is precisely opposite to the point I wish to argue since a view like Luther's leads unintentionally to spiritual frustration. If we believe that our ordinary work does not have any intrinsic value in the light of eternity, since it has nothing to do with heaven and will not be saved, then it has only a secondary, instrumental value for us. If, then, work is only a means to an end external to itself and our inner being, our work becomes cut off from who we are in our deepest selves. This alienates us from our work, and this alienation leads to frustration. As alien even to our "inner man," work can only have at best a secondary or second-level value. All callings other than the one to individual salvation may be equal on earth in one sense – they contribute nothing to our salvation. Yet, when we compare these callings among themselves, a group of higher callings nevertheless begins to emerge (like missionary or evangelist) because these are more obviously of penultimate value in relation to the "things of heaven."

This situation arises from Luther's new spirituality because, rather than destroying the dualistic hierarchy, he has relocated it between heaven and earth. The hierarchy used to be located between the contemplative and active life, where salvation was at stake. This obviously cut the masses off from justification. This new dualism, however, is between heavenly and earthly kingdoms. Luther was not able to totally dispense with the hierarchy of callings, despite any intentions he may have had to do so, because of his insistence on the distinction between the inner (spiritual) and outer (physical) man. Luther's distinction is just a different version of Pope John Paul II's dualism between person and things.

Although Luther would doubtless want to deny these implications, given what he elsewhere says so positively about work, theologically he cannot. With this doctrine he has boxed himself in. At the very least, this distinction Luther makes leads to confusion.

Thus Luther's theology has paradoxically and unintentionally introduced a new hierarchy of callings. Since all callings are now only earthly, even though through them we obediently love God and serve others in the freedom of salvation, most of us are now ultimately spending our lives working at things that, though valuable in this life, have nothing to do with eternity.

What happens when we find ourselves in a social situation different from that of Luther? What happens when, for example, as a part of growing up emotionally and spiritually we must discern "God's call" and choose our work? What happens when we must change our work due to circumstances beyond our control? Luther's theology does not help us and may actually confuse us. For, given the options of investing our lives in the things that at least address the inner man or the soul, and thus will last, or investing our lives in the things that obviously will pass away, most of us, if it were at all possible, would feel "called" to the former.

The theological reasoning here is relentless. We may go into a spiritual vocation, knowing it to be "first best" due to its correlation to eternity and therefore the higher calling. Or, if circumstances dictate otherwise, we will end up settling with working on things that will totally pass away, only indirectly if at all related to heaven. It is hard to avoid the conclusion that the latter are second best. But if we follow this latter course, having known that the alternative was there, we end up frustrated and wondering why God would not call us to work on the things that really matter. And our frustration will not go away simply because we tell ourselves that we should simply and obediently accept this "second best" option as God's providential call on our life.

If only those who are providentially called by God in their jobs to "preaching the gospel" – that is, to working toward things that are heavenly – are fortunate enough to be the Christians doing the important things, where does that leave the rest of us? While Luther cut out one hierarchy of callings with his new conception, in its place he inadvertently erected another. And it is this hierarchy of callings, carried on into evangelicalism, which lies at the heart of our view of work that simply does not work.

PART II

The Heavenly Future of Earthly Work

What Does the Bible Say?

3

Taking Earth to Heaven: The Resurrection

But our citizenship is in heaven. And we eagerly await a Savior from there, the Lord Jesus Christ, who, by the power that enables him to bring everything under his control, will transform our lowly bodies so that they will be like his glorious body.

Philippians 3:20–21

Part I cleared some theological and spiritual ground occupied by a few belief and piety structures that have led inadvertently to the spiritual frustration with daily work that so many Christians experience. While this destructive task made room for a new understanding of work that works theologically and practically, the questions and theological suggestions that steered that process are also tools for redeveloping the foundation upon which a new structure can be built. As any builder knows, the foundation is crucial. To the degree that we have so far been redeveloping the foundation, the construction of a new understanding of work is well underway.

Unless those steering questions and theological principles are the right tools for the job, however, our building will be in vain. These tools, or questions and principles, revolve primarily around a particular theological vision of the nature and scope of our future salvation. The fundamental question underlying this entire project concerns what God will and will not in the end take into eternity. What is the final destiny for the whole of this creation, physical and spiritual? And what conclusions related to spiritual meaning and Christian life in the world can be drawn from this?

The suggestion that salvation is the future not simply for souls but also for our bodies and the wider non-human creation as well – including within it our work – cannot simply be assumed in today's Christian landscape. For a very long time, popular Christianity has focused on salvation consisting of the immaterial soul going to heaven when we die. The belief that our ultimate salvation hope is the bodily resurrection to a transformed and genuinely physical new heaven and new earth has been relegated to the spiritual background, in danger of being lost altogether. The questions and assertions about the salvation of creation and about where deeper spiritual meaning lies need, then, to be tested biblically and theologically to prove their legitimacy.

It is likewise important for building the case for the heavenly good of earthly work that, through our theological interactions with Scripture, we consider carefully the other shaping principle behind this proposal – that is, for something to be valuable and thus full of meaning in the ultimate sense, it has to be "saved" and thus included in eternity.

What follows will test and explain these theological tools. The process will also establish a biblical context which makes it credible to suppose that our work carries forward into the new creation.

Interpreting Jesus' Resurrection

What from this universe, from what exists when Jesus returns and from what existed before that time, will God in the end save? Will it only be souls, or will it be physical entities as well? Will it include the non-human creation? And if so, will our work, now a legitimate part of creation, be caught up in this redeeming and healing transformation to the new creation?

As we will see, the Bible is quite clear on God's future promises for the physical creation – more so than some of us might have realized. It does not, however, state as literally as some might wish that what humans do in this life, specifically for our purposes "our work," will be included in this salvation. This lack of "proof-texts," however, does not mean that the Bible fails to teach such a view, or teach it clearly.

If we read the central New Testament texts on the resurrection and new creation in particular carefully and theologically, we will see that human work is *as much and to the same degree* an object of God's salvation as the rest of the material creation of which it is a part.[9] As we will see, the theology is there clearly in the texts as long as we know how to recognize it – even though the biblical writers are using this theology for different purposes to address specifically the pressing practical issues that they were facing.

This said, the first issue facing us is where in Scripture to begin. Should some passages have interpretative priority over others? Our starting point is crucial, for it is often the most significant factor shaping where we end up. But if choosing where to begin is simply a matter of theological preference, there is a real danger of theological circular reasoning creeping in and skewing the process – and thus our conclusions.

It is my understanding, along with much of the church throughout her history, that Jesus himself, his being and his work, is the interpretative lens for a Christian reading of Scripture (Lk. 24:44–45). The writers of the New Testament themselves practice this principle. For the New Testament reinterprets and transforms both the Scripture that we call the Old Testament and the whole of life, including the world around us, through the reality and story of Jesus' life, death and resurrection, ascension and future return in glory. Jesus, in his humanity and divinity, is the filter; the paradigm for seeing and understanding all of reality. Jesus is the archetype for both history and theology.

---

[9] For an extensive and scholarly examination of the physical nature of Jesus' resurrection, and thus our own promised resurrection, see N.T. Wright, *The Resurrection of the Son of God* (London: SPCK, 2003).

Given the questions at hand, then, we will reflect on a few prominent New Testament texts that focus in one way or another on Jesus' resurrection and thus our ultimate hope for salvation – the resurrection to the new creation which is the new heaven and the new earth. We will begin by setting the context with the narrative recounting Jesus' resurrection and ascension from Luke's Gospel. Following this we will examine further this principle, Jesus as salvation's paradigm – "Jesus as the quintessential Adam" – by considering Paul's theology of resurrection in both 1 Corinthians 15 and Colossians 1.

Romans 8, then, builds on this material by illustrating how this works out in God's promise for the future of the natural creation. This passage shows how Christ's destiny, as well as our own and that of nature, are bound up together. Finally, an examination of Revelation 21 and 22 round off our reflections with a closer look at the "*new* earth." There we will be able to tease out from the text several important aspects of human work that are envisioned as transformed and carrying over from this creation to the next.

Jesus the Prototype

Jesus himself *is* "the resurrection and the life" (Jn. 11:25). He is "the way the truth and the life" (Jn. 14:6). He is not simply our means of salvation; he is our salvation, our new life. Salvation is, as the Pauline letters repeatedly emphasize, being "in Christ" (2 Tim. 2:10; Rom. 3:24; 1 Cor. 1:30). When we are in Christ we become like Christ, and in this we are saved.

Thus, Jesus himself "in-[body]s" salvation. He is the paradigm or model of what salvation is and what we are to expect. The entitlements of divine Sonship and the life of God the Spirit come together in Jesus. In his very being, including his human physical body (risen and then ascended), he demonstrates to us what ultimately will be saved and what will not.

Throughout the New Testament this basic idea that Jesus is the embodiment, the very picture of salvation, is expressed in a number of meaningful images. In addition to those just mentioned, Jesus is in himself the actual "firstfruits" of salvation (1 Cor. 15:20, 23). He is the new or last Adam in whom truly human life – new and eternal life – exists in the flesh and from whom it flows to us (Rom. 5:14; 1 Cor. 15:22, 45). He is the prototype, or "firstborn," not just of creation (Col. 1:15), but also from the dead (Col. 1:18), and thus of those being conformed into his very likeness (Rom. 8:29). If we want to understand how to interpret biblically the extent and object of salvation we need to look at Jesus himself. The salvation and transformation of Jesus' body is the model for our salvation and also, as we will see, for the salvation of the cosmos. It thus tells us what we can expect to find and not to find (often expressed by theologians using the terms "continuity" and "discontinuity") in the new heaven and new earth.

Touch My Hands and Feet

As we begin to explore what Jesus' resurrection means for us by looking at the resurrection narrative in Luke's Gospel, an initial word of caution is in order. When we reflect on those physical properties carrying over from Jesus' earthly life into his resurrection life, we are technically not seeing Jesus' body in its *final* state of glory. We need to remember that neither Jesus' ascension nor his ultimate glorification have yet taken place.

Jesus' post-resurrection appearances and activities thus take place uniquely, straddling current "earthly" and future "heavenly" corporeal worlds. As we will see in Revelation 21 and 22, when the new creation fully comes both heaven and earth will be fully brought together. Here in these appearances of Jesus, however, we find only a foretaste anticipating what that fulfillment will be.

Thus, Jesus' body in these narratives lives uniquely within the physics of both this world and whatever the physics will be in the world to come. All the same, as we will see, Jesus clearly has the same body. But it's a body with additional, transformed properties.

This caution notwithstanding, we also need to be careful not to pass over too quickly what we find carrying over from Jesus' earthly life into his resurrected life. For "this same Jesus" who appeared and then ascended into heaven will *in the same way* come back (Acts 1:11). And we need to remember that in his final glory Jesus will appear bodily as the "lamb slain" (Rev. 5:6). Thus, to posit too radical a discontinuity between the post-resurrection form of Jesus' body and his ascended and finally glorified bodily form would seem as unwise as positing too simplistic a continuity.

The importance of these observations will become clearer as we look into our biblical texts. For the pattern we discover here we will see again, first used by Paul to guide his own theological vision of our hoped for resurrection and creation's ultimate salvation. Likewise, we will find the same pattern mirrored in John's vision of the new heaven and new earth at the end of Revelation.

But let's turn now to the narrative itself. The account of Jesus' resurrection and appearances in Luke 24 begins at Jesus' empty tomb. As the women arrive there early on Sunday morning they are surprised to find that Jesus is missing. They have come with spices (to preserve Jesus' dead body from further decay) but are shocked to find that the stone sealing him in has been rolled away. Verse 3 states that the actual physical body of Jesus is gone. Even while the women are trying to figure out what might have happened, "two men" appear to them and announce (v. 6) that Jesus is missing because he has risen – just like he told them he would.

Note here a few important details. What might be the purpose of the stone having been rolled away? Why would this be necessary, and why is it a focal point in the narrative? From what we learn in other accounts of Jesus' resurrection, the stone didn't have to be rolled away. It would have been easy for Jesus simply to pass through it while it was still in place. As we find recorded in John 20:26, there was something new about Jesus' resurrected body that allowed him to pass through solid objects, like closed doors.

Yet this text, like John 20, emphasizes that the stone has been rolled away. Why? Because it points out to us that the risen Son has not discarded his genuinely physical and material existence. He has not in death and resurrection transcended physical existence and become a "spirit." His "soul" is not what gets saved. For Jesus, salvation extends new life to his whole human life and not simply to his divine or spiritual aspects. Jesus is the same person with the same body who was killed and buried. God the Son, the second person of the Trinity, retains this same physical body for all eternity.

The stone is our first clue in the text that specifically highlights the continuity between Jesus' body from his earthly life and his resurrected eternal body. Although Jesus might have been able to pass through the stone, he did not. This fact demonstrates the essential place of the created *physical* realm in God's salvation purposes.

Yet continuity is not the whole story. Verse 13 records the scene on the road to Emmaus, Jesus' first appearance to two other followers. And here a striking aspect of discontinuity (possibly physical) is emphasized.

We are told in verse 14 that when Jesus approached, and then spent an extended time talking with these followers, they failed to recognize him – or were "kept from recognizing him" (v. 16). The text does not record what exactly kept them from recognizing him. Was it cognitive dissonance at an extremely stressful time? Was it God himself supernaturally withholding from them the ability to see that it was Jesus? Or might there have been something different or new about his appearance?

The text is oddly silent on this matter and, it appears, leaves us to ponder this quite natural question. Regardless of the answer, the point of the story at this place in the narrative seems to be to emphasize something new, to show that Jesus' resurrected body was more than a mere resuscitation from the dead. Something was different about Jesus to the extent that his close followers, for whatever reason, were not able to recognize him.

However, when Jesus eventually took bread, gave thanks, and broke it (continuity to show that it was indeed him), their eyes were opened and they fully recognized him physically (v. 31). And at this point they realized that they had in fact somewhat recognized him already while on the road (v. 32).

Following this, Jesus "disappeared from their sight" (v. 31). Jesus appears again, however – this time to the Eleven (v. 36). Although at first they thought that they had seen a "ghost" (whether due to shock or to a slight difference in Jesus' appearance, v. 37), Jesus points out to them the continuity between his risen body and the one they last saw. "Why are you troubled, and why do doubts rise in your minds? Look at my hands and my feet. It is I myself! Touch me and see; a ghost does not have flesh and bones, as you see I have" (vv. 38–39).

Then, as if this were not enough to demonstrate that his very same physical body had been raised, Jesus took and ate a piece of broiled fish in their presence (v. 43). And it was only then, having fully established that he himself was bodily raised, that Scripture in all its details began to make sense to the disciples (vv. 44–49). Indeed, this was the beginning of Jesus' followers, here under his own instruction, understanding that he is the prototype, the grid through which all reality, Scripture, and even salvation, should be interpreted.

After this, the text somewhat abruptly concludes with Jesus blessing them and then ascending (vv. 50–51). The impact on us of this rather sudden ending is probably much the same as it would have been on the disciples. We, and they, are left to wonder and reflect on what we have just seen and experienced. And, for many throughout the history of the church, possibly the most prominent aspect of this account to ponder is that the risen and thus healed – and now immortal and incorruptible bodily Jesus – still bears the nail scars in his hands and feet.[10] Jesus' invitation to see and touch his hands and his feet makes it clear that the scars are the focus. Indeed, the text leaves it to our imaginations to touch and feel for ourselves.

The theological point, however, is as striking as the emotional impact. Jesus, God the Son, does – and will for all eternity – have a physical human body that bears the marks received during his bodily existence in this life. Humanity in this instance, even (or especially) in something as vile as our sin, has "added something" through our actions permanently to eternity; the crucifixion was a "work" carried out by many people. We have made an imprint on Jesus' (God's) eternal physical body. And since this body, still containing those scars, is now ascended back into the Godhead, the results of at least this particular "human work" are guaranteed to carry over into God's as well as our own future and eternal reality. For he will return in glory even as the Lamb slain.

That he is the Lamb slain from the creation of the world (Rev. 13:8) challenges neither our observation nor its implications. For this does not mean that Jesus' body existed either outside time or in eternity past "already scarred." It means that the Son's disposition has always included his willingness to give himself for us.

Yet is it only through our sinful "work" that we shape or add to what ultimately continues into eternity? Or is this instance of our "shaping eternity" through our actions an exception, a unique event in the unique history of salvation and in the unique life of Christ?

No. As we will now see, other New Testament writers make it clear that they see in Jesus a pattern, a principle that through his body he is the prototype for the coming new creation. And they show that, in the same way as Jesus' resurrection, God will ultimately transform evil, neutral, and good aspects of creation for his purposes. That this transformation includes our work

---

[10] This is also true, and probably more so, in the similar account in John's Gospel 20:25–27.

on creation, just like it did our "work" on Jesus, naturally follows.

Quintessentially Adam

That the resurrected Jesus embodies our future hope as the pattern for our salvation and that of all of creation is a consistent pastoral principle for the Apostle Paul. To illustrate how Paul builds his theology, and to enable us to grasp better its implications for the heavenly future of our ordinary work, we reflect now on a few texts from Paul's letters that demonstrate most vividly his theology and method.

Shortly we will examine Romans 8, where the cosmic scope of resurrection – Jesus', ours, and the whole of the physical creation's – is shown most unambiguously to be bound together and to be the ultimate Christian hope. This text will shed a great deal of light on our question about the future of our work.

Firstly, however, we turn to 1 Corinthians 15 and Colossians 1. In these texts Paul sets out his understanding of Jesus as our prototype (the one in whose person earth is taken to heaven), and he uses this hope and pattern to encourage believers to persevere in their lives and "work." As we will see, for Paul, the strength to carry on in daily life comes from the hope that who we are and what we do in this life has a heavenly, resurrected future. For Paul, that which is ultimately valuable, and thus leads to meaning in this life, is that which is included in the resurrection and is thus eternal. The question is this: Is this "work" indeed "of the Lord" and can it legitimately be understood to apply to our ordinary as well as to our "religious" work?

Throughout 1 Corinthians 15 Paul develops a nuanced theological argument concerning our resurrection hope, the hope of salvation, in order to help us find purpose and meaning in what he specifically calls the "Lord's work." (Our question, of course, is what kind of work does this include?) Following his extended reflections – firstly on the resurrection of Christ, secondly on our resurrection which follows the same pattern, and thirdly on the specific nature of the bodily and physical resurrection we are to expect – Paul urges, "Stand firm. Let nothing move you. Always give yourselves fully to the work of the Lord, because you know that your labor in the Lord is not in vain" (v. 58).

Of course, in the context of 1 Corinthians 15 Paul's overall purpose is to help the believers resist false teaching and beliefs that undermine the fact and meaning of the resurrection – the gospel. He summarizes, "If Christ has not been raised, your faith is futile; you are still in your sins . . . [and] lost. If only for this life we have hope in Christ, we are to be pitied" (vv. 17–19). Here our faith is clearly hope that we, too, following the pattern of Christ, will be raised and transformed into our own immortal bodily existence (vv. 35-56).

Paul's point is that without the bodily resurrection, our faith is useless (v. 14). For without this heavenly hope, nothing in or about this life, physically or spiritually, is meaningful. Without the resurrection that preserves and transforms the physical body, life itself is lost because our whole existence is only fleeting, it is subject to the "sting of death" (v. 55) and thus is perishable (v. 54).

Thus, as presented in this context, our "labor in the Lord," the "work of the Lord," refers most directly to the hard work needed to understand, hold onto, and witness to Christ's and our own resurrection. Yet is this all that Paul's phrase "labor in the Lord" legitimately applies to?

The church has never been inclined to think that the "work of the Lord" only includes sound teaching specifically about the resurrection. Indeed, we have always taken the principle in this verse to refer more widely to all that we do in the power of the Spirit relating to the good news of Christ. The question is whether this applies only to so-called "religious" activities. We return to the question we asked in Chapter 1: What really constitutes God's work? What counts for the "work of the Lord"? Is it only narrowly conceived religious activities or is it also ordinary working activities in which we engage "under God" and with his strength?

Although some might be inclined to see "labor in the Lord" or the Lord's work only as what we traditionally call "spiritual" ministry, nothing in the text necessarily limits our participation and witness to the resurrection to narrowly "religious" working activity. Indeed, getting away from a narrow view of what is "spiritual" that downplays physical life seems to be the whole point of Paul's teaching on the physical resurrection. Showing how the spiritual and physical come together in the resurrection (and how this transforms our understanding of what might commonly be thought about both) is this text's point – not the ordering of "spirit" over "matter." How so?

Paul does call the Corinthian believers foolish for asking how the dead are raised and "With what kind of body will they come?" (v. 36). Yet, he does not rebuke them for *enquiring* about how the resurrected body incorporates both the spiritual and the physical. Were this his point he wouldn't have gone on to answer just that question so directly. Rather, Paul is apparently chastising these believers for asking the question cynically, as if this question didn't matter or, worse yet, as if such a resurrection is not possible.

To counter such reckless and spiritually dangerous skepticism, in verses 36–39 Paul explains the nature and reasonableness, in God's way of things, of the idea of the resurrection body. He does this by emphasizing, with analogies from nature, the integral, natural or continuous relationship between our current body and the one to come. "What you sow does not come to life unless it dies. When you sow, you do not plant the body that will be, but just a seed" (vv. 36–37). What is interesting to notice, however, is that the new body is not a replacement body coming out of thin air, but rather one that comes from and is organically related to, a fulfillment of, the one that dies. God has indeed created things so that even by observing the order of nature we can see the logic and necessity of resurrection – a seed of wheat produces a body of wheat in the future (vv. 37–38).

Whether verse 40, speaking of heavenly bodies, is talking specifically about the resurrection body, or whether it continues the illustration from nature, might be debated. From the context, bringing us back around to the "resurrection of the dead" only in verse 42, it seems clear that the earthly/heavenly body distinctions here are simply a continuation of his illustration from nature. Paul does not seem here to be contrasting the physics of this creation and the new creation. These verses show that there is continuity, a genuine carryover between that which dies and that which is resurrected. The new body is the same "in kind" as the first.

Yet even if I am wrong and the reference to earthly/heavenly bodies is intended to be contrasted, all that this distinction would show is the important parallel principle of discontinuity. All that it would be saying is that our new body will need to be transformed from the way it is in this present life (characterized by death and decay) to be fitted to the conditions in the new creation. Indeed, this is the point later of Paul's contrasts in verses 50–56 between perishable/imperishable and mortal/immortal bodies.

In those verses Paul does bring out critical aspects of discontinuity between the natural and raised body. And this principle, as seen in Luke's narrative as well, will become vital for us to consider later when we think through the judgement and transformation of our work which is part of the natural world currently subject to decay. For if Christ's transformation, and thus our transformation, is prototypical of what creation can expect, then what is true of the change needed from the natural to the spiritual body also applies to the transformation of the non-human creation. But we will explore this more later.

That the new body is "imperishable" rather than "perishable" (v. 53), that imperishability requires a body taking us beyond our current "flesh and blood" physics (v. 50) makes it clear that resurrection takes us far beyond brute biological resuscitation. A genuine transformation in our physics must take place for resurrection to fit us for eternity. This is what I like to refer to as the "new physics" that will characterize the new heaven and earth. As Paul says, we must "all be changed – in a flash" (v. 51–52) for immortal life to be possible.

The fact that resurrection is not simply a reviving from the dead is important. The transience of all things, including the decay that sets into living things quickly after death, means that something more than resuscitation is required. Resurrection does, of course, give life back (or extend God's life) to what has died/decayed. But it also involves so much more, and this "yes but more" dynamic characterizing our principle of continuity and discontinuity, when thinking about the resurrected body, serves as more than just an interesting fact about bodily resurrection. It is also an interpretative tool that will help us later in our broader constructive purposes concerning work.

Yet so we do not get bogged down here, and begin to think that Paul is (or indeed we are) simply speculating vainly on things beyond human knowledge, we need to remember that Paul's explanation of the nature of the resurrection body is nothing more than an extended reflection on the resurrected Jesus himself,who is our prototype. And to help him draw this idea out, Paul uses here what for him has become a frequently used device, the Adam/Christ model.

Parallel to the theology in Romans 5:14 (and to what we will see in a moment in Colossians 1), where Adam is referred to as "the pattern of the one to come," in two places here in 1 Corinthians 15 Paul specifically turns to the Adam/Christ dynamic to show how Jesus is the archetype encapsulating our future resurrection. This dynamic is important because theologically it is the means of expression Paul uses to unite earth to heaven, matter to spirit, and us to Christ. How so?

In 1 Corinthians 15:20 Paul refers to the resurrected Jesus as the "firstfruits" from among the dead. This concept, borrowed from the Hebrew Scriptures, highlights Jesus' similarity to, or continuity with, those who will follow him from the dead in the resurrection. The term "firstfruits" alone would have made the point that Jesus is the model for those that will be saved.

Yet in order to show what this means and thus to make this paradigmatic linkage even clearer, Paul continues, "For since death came through a man, the resurrection of the dead comes also through a man. For as in Adam all die, so in Christ all will be made alive. But each in his own turn: Christ, the firstfruits; then, when he comes, those who belong to him" (vv. 21–23).

Yet this salvation, this work of Christ, does not stop with saving people, soul and body. The Lord's work of resurrection encompasses realities far beyond what we usually think of as objects of "religious" interest. It brings with it the transformation of all realities, what we might call "secular realities." For here, in bringing resurrection to his own, Christ likewise brings "everything" under his feet (v. 27); presumably purifying them by destroying death (v. 26) and "all dominion, authority and power" characterized by death that thus stands against him (v. 24). Here there is no distinction between the spiritual and what is natural – everything is included in the work of the Lord.

Nor, importantly, does this destruction of dominion, authority, and power equate to annihilating non-religious realities beyond Christ and people. If that were the case there would be nothing left to be under his feet, or for God to be "all in all" in relation to.

Indeed Christ's work is parallel to, though much more than, the work of the first Adam (who we will look at in Chapter 4). Christ's work involves bringing "everything," all of creation, both the spiritual and secular, under his Lordship. Jesus' spiritual work in resurrection has as much to do with transforming mundane and even hostile earthly realities as it does the religious aspects of life. Indeed, the "Lord's work" here includes everything so that in the end "God may be all in all" (v. 28).

Certainly the point to be emphasized here is that Christ's work is about gathering up and taking into/under God all that exists in this creation. That this "everything" that exists will include what we have added to creation through our "working" seems evident, though this too will need to be purged of all evil – the power and remnants of death – like everything else. Of course (vv. 29ff.), if there is no bodily resurrection – for Christ, for people and for creation alike – neither religious life nor ordinary life like eating and drinking (the work to produce these products implied) make any sense theoretically or practically.

The second reference in 1 Corinthians 15 to the Adam/Christ dynamic comes in verse 45. At this point, simply to add greater substance to our point, we will look briefly at what we find here.

The first Adam (a living being from the "dust of the earth," vv. 45, 47) and the last Adam (a life-giving spirit, "the second man from Heaven," vv. 45, 48) are both fully and physically human. This is why they are fitting parallels. The last Adam, however, while gathering up and embodying everything pertaining to the first, is much more. Jesus post-resurrection does not replace the material Adam by becoming a ghost or phantasm. Luke makes this clear in his resurrection account. But he does bring together the spiritual and the physical into one new reality in a way that we too will experience one day. As Paul says referring to our prototype Jesus, the last Adam, "just as we have borne the likeness of the earthly man, so shall we bear the likeness of the man from heaven" (v. 49).

Now this teaching, bringing together the human/material and the divine/spiritual in the one man Jesus Christ, to be the achievement and fulfillment of Adam (humanity), is absolutely crucial to Paul's whole theology of salvation. And this is why salvation hope has to be for a physical resurrection. For, without the salvation of the material as well as the spiritual, Adam and all of earthly existence are lost, not saved. Were resurrection to be of spirit, giving it the priority and ultimate worth over matter, then creation (including humanity) would not in the end truly be saved. It would be done away with and replaced.

In order to look even more deeply into this cosmic vision of physical salvation, so that we can grasp what it means for the future of our work, we will examine how, in Romans 8, Paul builds what we might call "inclusive layers" within the resurrection. This means that creation's salvation is included "in us" (Adam/humanity) as we are included "in Christ" (Adam/creation's head). Yet to help us grasp how this will work, we want first to take a brief look at Colossians 1:15–23.

The main point we want to notice, from this parallel discussion to 1 Corinthians 15, is how Paul focuses on the Adam/Christ dynamic in salvation in order to bind together the material to the spiritual, the secular to the religious. In Colossians 1:15–23, Paul through that dynamic shows how it can be that Christ "by" his "physical body" (v. 22) is the salvation hope for believers, and "the gospel" for "every creature under heaven" (v. 23).

Beginning in Colossians 1:15, Paul sets up his argument by painting a picture of Jesus as the true Adam. "He [Christ] is the image of the invisible God, the firstborn over all creation." While Adam was created *in order* to image God, Christ is said *in fact* to image, or to be the "icon" of, the invisible God. Jesus is the fulfillment of Adam, the man made to reflect, or image, God. And as the new Adam, he is the model, or archetype, for what it means now and for eternity to be truly human.

Yet at the same time Jesus shows us, in his humanity, who God is and what God is like. "For God was pleased to have all his fullness dwell in him, and through him to reconcile to himself all things" (vv. 19–20). In himself, through his incarnation, Jesus unites fully (and thus saves) that which is spirit and that which is matter – all things secular, or earthly, and all things religious, or heavenly.

As such, Jesus is called the fulfilled "firstborn" over the whole of the physical creation. This is, of course, because initially he created "all things," and, similar to the first Adam, all things were created "for" him (v. 16). Jesus also holds "all things" together. As we will see, he fulfills the first Adam's calling to image God in his work (v. 17).

But this alone is not sufficient to unite fully creation ("all things") and us to Christ. The new Adam, Jesus, is also truly "the head of the body, the church" (v. 18). And because of this "he is the beginning and firstborn from among the dead" (v. 18). He is the prototype for creation and for believers, and thus he unites both in salvation. Through his self, the fulfillment or perfection of humanity is achieved and salvation is brought – not just to the church or humans, but also in the same way to the whole of the cosmos "whether things on earth or things in heaven, by making peace through his blood shed on the cross" (v. 20). Indeed, Jesus takes earth – and all the things within it – to heaven.

The theology concerning the future salvation for creation is here unambiguous. All that is saved, reconciled by Christ's physical body (v. 22), becomes holy in his sight (v. 22). Whatever this applies to, human and cosmic, is thus shown by God's saving actions to be of ultimate (final) worth or value to him – and therefore these things should also be of such value to us.

The Future of Creation, God's and Ours (Romans 8)

When explaining the stages of salvation, theologians will often refer to the final state, or end, of salvation as the ultimate (future) glorification. When we talk or sing about "glorification" in church we usually focus upon Jesus. We seldom think of "glory" in relation to ourselves or the natural world.

Yet Romans 8 teaches that the whole creation participates in glorification, too – through resurrection. Although this might seem odd at first, once we understand how human and non-human glorification is necessarily a part of Jesus' own glorification, then God's ultimate purpose for creation (as we will see graphically in Revelation 21–22) becomes more understandable. Let me explain.

Romans 8:1 begins by declaring boldly that for those of us "in Christ Jesus" there is "now no condemnation." Our glorification (the opposite of condemnation, vv. 17–18), which is also our freedom (v. 2), is possible because the Son took on a physical way of life that is modeled in the "likeness of sinful man" (v. 3). And as our representative, Jesus then became for us a sin offering (v. 3) so that the "righteous requirements of the law" would be fully met (v. 4). But, interestingly, these requirements are not met – we might have expected the text to say "in him." Rather, righteousness is met "in us" who now live according to the Spirit (v. 4). The text begins, of course, with the condition that firstly we must be "in Christ" (v. 1), "in accordance with the Spirit" (v. 5).

As puzzling as this may seem, it is in fact this "layering," or multiple levels of inclusion using the preposition "in," that becomes the key to understanding the theology of resurrection contained in this text. Thus it is also the key to understanding the future hope of creation (v. 21). The importance of this "inclusive layering" will become clearer, however, as we explore further.

If we skip ahead in the text, down to verses 9–10, we find that we who are controlled by the Spirit, who have the Spirit of Christ "in" us, though our "body is dead" (subject to the principle of death) "due to sin," nevertheless our "spirit is alive." However, lest we be tempted to think that this implies the ultimate triumph or priority of spirit over matter, in verse 11 Paul says that if we have the Spirit "in" us, "he who raised Christ from the dead will also give life to [our] mortal bodies."

And why is this important? Because without our physical resurrection, there is no hope for the wider non-human creation, and thus salvation would be incomplete and Christ would not truly be God's "heir" to creation (v. 17).

At the end of a quite important section on "sonship" (vv. 12–17),[11] we find the first direct promise that we who are mere creatures will "share in his [Christ's] glory." Immediately following, in verse 18, we find what again might seem strange to us at first. The future glory which is Christ's will be revealed

[11] We will look at this section more fully in Chapter 5.

not directly by Jesus, but rather indirectly through or, as the text says, "in us."[12] But how is this possible?

Beginning in verse 19, we see that the whole creation "waits in eager expectation" for its salvation. Non-human reality is also the object of God's final salvation and will be vindicated and thus *justified* in being ultimately valuable. For effect here, though, and to emphasize creation's genuine right to salvation, Paul personifies this natural but non-human world. He describes it as waiting, even groaning (v. 22), in frustration (v. 20) because it is trapped in bondage to decay – permeated by sin and death (v. 21).

According to verse 21, however, the salvation/liberation of the material (here non-human) universe does not come as we might have expected, directly through Christ at his glorious return. Rather, salvation will come to the whole of the non-human creation only when "brought into the glorious freedom of the children of God" which is, as verse 23 states, the "redemption of our bodies."

Of course our resurrection only comes to us "in Christ." But the text is careful here to make *our* redemption the focus and the gateway to the redemption guaranteed to the rest of the physical creation.

This ordering here: creation is "in us" as we are "in Christ," is quite important theologically. The non-human creation, of course, did not fall into sin by its own choice. Apparently, here in reference to Genesis 3, it is God, "in hope that the creation itself will be liberated," who "subjected [creation] to frustration" (vv. 20–21). But why would God tie creation's glorious destiny to human choice and destiny? In what way is the non-human creation "in" humanity?

---

12 It is possible to translate this phrase "to us," as in the NRSV, rather than "in us" (so NIV). However, the context here emphasizes throughout our inclusion "in Christ" or "in the Spirit." Thus the theological flow of the text, tying creation's redemption into our resurrection, suggests that "in us" is the best translation.

This is where the Adam/Christ dynamic that we explored earlier helps us out. Adam, of course, was firstly a natural creation himself, from "the dust of the earth." He is necessarily bound up with, and a part of, the physical creation. Yet he was also given a special calling within creation to be more – to be God's image, or responsible representative (a concept we will examine more closely in Chapter 4). Because of his unique identity uniting both heaven (the image of God) and earth (the rest of creation), when Adam fell spiritually he took with him that to which he was joined naturally, as a physical being, and thus that which he was responsible for – the non-human creation. And in this same way, as we have seen in Colossians and 1 Corinthians, the salvation brought by the last Adam, Christ, must also extend to the rest of the material creation.

Yet Romans 8, rather than focusing on Christ in this function, focuses on us instead. It is we who are "in Christ," and thus also now the new humanity (the image of God completed), who take on the role, as we justly should, of bringing the non-human creation to its glorification, or "glorious" destiny.

Creation's salvation hope, then, its "liberation" (v. 21), is that it will be brought or ushered "in us" into our own glory, which is our physical resurrection "in Christ." Since nature co-inheres "in us," our salvation and glorification become creation's own salvation and glory.

That this salvation of the natural world includes our work follows logically. Work, which has further shaped nature, is now just as much a part of nature as what God made originally. Unless we want to understand work itself to be "un-natural," a result of the curse (we will see in Chapter 4 that it never was) then, purged of its cursed laboriousness, we must conclude from this biblical material that our work experiences salvation along with us.

If this is correct, however, we would expect to find such a vision elsewhere in Scripture too. And indeed, when we look at Revelation 21 and 22, this is just what we find. Here, through a careful reading of the text, we discern that the coming glory does in fact preserve and transform what humans have done in creation through our work.[13]

Transforming Work (Revelation 21 and 22)

So what in John's vivid description of the new creation do we find carried over from this creation? Are there indeed products of human culture? Whatever we discover here we would expect, of course, to square with what we have learned concerning Jesus' own body, and with what we have learned from Paul's understanding of resurrection.

Yet, throughout Christian history, many have suggested that the coming salvation involves an annihilation of this earth that human beings have ruined. Those following this view envision heaven as replacing earth and prefer to think of the new heaven and earth as simply a return to Eden (materially or non-materially), to God's pristine creation untouched by human hands. So what do we observe in Revelation 21 and 22?

Naturally, the descriptions of the new creation in this text are not presented as "facts" to fuel our "end-time" fantasies. Rather, they are guiding illustrations for our communities of faith to stimulate our own, now "sanctified," theological imaginations.

God's people, of course, have always been invited to engage in this kind of imaginative theology. In the Old Testament, various visions prophesying the life to come when the Messiah arrived led the people of God forward. And although these Old Testament visions are still completely appropriate for us, they were specifically cast according to Israel's hope, and in ways that made sense of concrete realities in their lives.

When Israel's hope is realized, for example, their normal life activities (including their ability to traverse and farm the land

---

[13] For a fuller treatment of this see my *A Theology of Work*, 136–51. See also Richard Bauckham, *The Theology of the Book of Revelation* (Cambridge: CUP, 1993).

which is part of their identity) will be a breeze since the curse making their work laborious will be lifted. For then "Every valley shall be raised up, every mountain and hill made low; the rough ground shall become level, the rugged places a plain" (Isa. 40:4). Likewise, their hope that human and non-human life will live together in *shalom*, in harmony rather than in strife, will become a reality (Isa. 11:8; 65:25).

Yet because of Christ's coming, it is the New Testament's description of the new heaven and new earth, presented in the midst of great frustration and pressure for God's people, that concerns us here. Appropriately, this fullest vision of our hope is found at the end of Scripture, in the book of Revelation. Further, it comes to us in the literary form most suited to this kind of hopeful theological thinking – apocalyptic.

As apocalyptic vision, like the rest of the book, Revelation 21 and 22 are not meant to be read as what we might think of today as a video or photographic image of the future new creation. The vision is completely truthful in what it says, of course, and the future it directs us toward is a real, concrete, embodied existence – not an imaginary fairytale or myth. Nevertheless its purpose, as apocalyptic, is descriptive rather than prescriptive. It serves *somewhat* like today's sophisticated science fiction should – as a paradigm or model for the imagination. It is meant to stimulate within us, and along certain tramlines, the courage needed in this life to envision and enact new ways of living, to resist evil and endure in spite of it, to live differently in its midst with hope rather than fear. We know that ultimately our resistance is not futile, and that eventually the whole of our lives will be vindicated and justified by God himself.

Thus, the imagery here does not answer abstractly our more speculative questions concerning what exactly we will or will not find in eternity. However, if interpreted modestly and in the context of pastoral encouragement (given our frustrations as workers), the visions of a heavenly Jerusalem, city of God, and "garden city" illustrate the characteristic nature and ethos of eternity. That is, these visions reveal something of the contours of both God's and our own eternal future.

Revelation 21 begins with the vision of a new heaven and a new earth (v. 1). To be more specific, it offers a vision of heaven and earth – which in the initial creation were distinct, and at times seemed to be mirror opposites of one another – merging together in the new future. In this vision the dwelling place of God and the dwelling place of humanity are one new "city," one new integrated reality that is home for both God and humanity, spirit and matter (v. 3).

The image of the "heavenly Jerusalem" emphasizes this unity – and both its continuity and discontinuity with this creation (v. 2). So, for example, unlike this creation, the new creation has no sea – which in this context symbolizes destructive evil, the possibility of the reversion to chaos (v. 1).[14] It is also "new" because now, unlike even the Garden of Eden before the Fall, all persons of the triune God will live continually and permanently in it with us (v. 3). Fear will cease since there will be no more pain or loss. Indeed, death itself and all that flows from it will be gone. A "new creation order" will thus have arrived (v. 4) – one in which the presence of Christ himself does not replace, but rather *makes*, everything new (v. 5).

Jesus himself is this salvation. He is "the Alpha and the Omega, the Beginning and the End" (v. 6). And although the historical temple (the location and thus promise of God's full presence) will be missing, it will nevertheless be present in Jesus himself. His body will embody the temple and, as the presence and glory of God, he will enable us to see things the way they really are so that we can appropriately live out our new life in his presence (vv. 22–23).

Yet the New Jerusalem is not only a divine city, heaven coming to earth. It is also quite earthly. It is depicted as the bride, the wife of the Lamb (v. 9). It is thus the creation, but the perfected and glorified creation (vv. 15–21) that has been taken by

[14] Richard Bauckham, *Book of Revelation*, 53.

Christ to heaven. Here it is expressed as the fullness of saved humanity (and thus the cosmos therein?) symbolized by the 12 tribes of Israel and the 12 apostles (vv. 12–14).

It is also, importantly for its inhabitants, a city of glorious possibilities. It will be forever open (v. 25) to include the best of human culture (achievements past and possibly ongoing). And although this is not in any way limited to our work, it will thus include what we have accomplished through work. For what we have done, our "splendor," will be brought and put on display as part of the "glory and honor of the nations" (vv. 24–26). Of course, even though it is open, nothing or no one still permeated by the old order of things will be allowed to enter (v. 27). Only what has been purified in Christ and listed in his book of life will find its freedom (cf. Rom. 8).

That there is genuine continuity between the current and future creation and that humanity, and not simply God, shapes its new reality is further vividly expressed through the very image chosen to describe this new heaven and new earth. The image is a city. One might have thought that the pre-Fall Garden of Eden, what God created alone, would have been a more fitting image. Although many Christians have thought that heaven is simply a return to Eden, this is not the case in this vision. Here a city, at best an ambivalent product of human work (Gen. 4:17), represents the future of God's and our new created reality.

But this is more than just any city; it is called Jerusalem, the city of God. Even this is at best an ambivalent symbol for Christians. For, although Jerusalem is a symbol and place of spiritual hope throughout the Bible, it nevertheless became a place of terror for Christians since humanity crucified Christ there.

Both as city and as Jerusalem, the new creation is a transformed and now holy place (v. 2). The vision suggests that God is pleased to gather up, transform, and include not just his "pure" creation, but also the genuine additions to the created reality that we have brought about through creation-transforming actions.

Jesus' nail-scarred hands and feet are the prototype for the coming new creation. What we find true in his body, we also find true in this vision. What we have done – although it is ambivalent at best on its own – once redeemed and transformed does find a home in the new creation.

Of course, God does still gather up and take into the new creation his own pristine creation. And he gives it a central place. Chapter 22 adds a clear reference to the garden – the "river of the water of life" (v. 1) with the "tree of life" beside it (v. 2) – to the vision. Yet here the garden is not fenced off but stands in the middle of the city to make the city what it is – a place of life and healing (v. 2). This garden city gathers up and preserves within it the glory of the unspoiled creation. Here nature is not destroyed or replaced but set free.

In this city characterized by healing and life (v. 2), even the nations (human political creations) find their restoration and fulfillment. Unlike the first garden, there is no cursed condition.

Thus salvation, the new creation, includes and preserves – but is also much more (through transformation) than the garden ever was. We have seen this principle again and again – transformation grounded in the very body of the resurrected Jesus.

One powerful description of our salvation to the new creation is found in the Advent hymn "Joy to the World": "Joy to the earth, the Savior reigns! . . . He comes to make his blessings flow/Far as the curse is found."

In the next chapter we will examine the nature and scope of this curse and its connection with our work. Before we do that, however, we need to understand the four-fold nature of salvation to be found in the new heaven and new earth.

Firstly, the new creation is a place where the relationship between God and humans is restored as a constant and full friendship.

Secondly, it is a place where the relationships between people are fully restored and are fully co-operative and harmonious.

Thirdly, it is a place where each person is fully healed and experiences well-being, a harmonious relationship within him or herself. Each person's human potential is realized. It is a place where we become, as we will see in the next chapter, what we were always intended to be.

And, fourthly, the new heaven and new earth is a place where God, humanity, and the rest of creation come together to experience harmony and intimacy in mutual relationships appropriate to each, and for the glory and flourishing of each. This is the meaning of the eternal Sabbath rest for God, humanity, and creation. God is at home and creation is released to live the life, human and non-human, that God had always envisioned for it. It is a place of true community where creation itself is included in the life-giving relationships of the triune God.

4

The Original Job Description: God's Apprentices (Genesis 1 – 11)

For we are God's workmanship, created in Christ Jesus to do good works, which God prepared in advance for us to do.

Ephesians 2:10

Where Do I Fit in God's Story?

The vision we have seen of God's re-creativity, of our coming salvation to the new creation, is mind-blowing. Were Christians to paint pictures of a future like this for those outside the faith, most would at least admit that ours is a compelling and alluring hope for today's world.

Yet have you ever wondered, despite God's desire to save us, *why* he might have made us to begin with? Have you ever considered *what* God might have made us for? Many Christians will respond almost intuitively that God created us to worship him. That is, he created us *for his* glory and *for his* own good pleasure. But is it only "all about God" and "not about me" as many of us today so passionately sing? Is there not, in God's purposes, a reason for our existence *pertaining to us*?

To make it clear that human existence also has purpose and meaning for our own sakes, Christians in the Reformed tradition would add that humanity's "chief end" includes *our* enjoying God forever. But what does this mean?

As we have seen, humanity's end, or God's final design for us, includes our being brought, through his permanent presence with us, into a fully mature and harmonious relationship with him. But is there anything behind this existential condition of relationship that might tell us more about who God intended us to be? Is a relationship with God a "purpose" in itself? Or does it also make other things possible?

Had God created us *simply* for the sake of a perfected relationship with himself, he could easily have created us in that final state. But he didn't. Even from the beginning and before sin, God's presence and fellowship with humanity was not full or uninterrupted – it was limited to his evening visits in the garden. Why did God create us this way, rather than in the final state? Why did he create creatures with potential and room, indeed even a need, to grow?

Some Christians argue, and others at least suggest by the way they tell the Christian story, that God created us *primarily* so that he could send Christ to save us. If that were so, however, that might suggest that our fall is required within the plot – and even, therefore, that God himself wrote it into the story. This would mean, however, that God had to cause, or in some way guarantee or bring about, our fall into sin in order to achieve his ultimate purposes. Although we might prefer to think that God only indirectly brought this about through our own fault, rather than causing it directly himself, a story recounting God's purposes for us that requires our fall into sin so that he could save us sounds suspect, even perverse. Nor does it really answer our question regarding why we are here.

Maybe, therefore, we weren't created first and foremost to be redeemed. Maybe the story is different. Maybe God created us for something else, for some other glory that we *now* need to be brought back or redeemed to. The question, then, becomes twofold: How and why does salvation restore us to the place we fell from (our initial purpose)? And how does salvation also take us beyond our beginning to where God always intended to bring us (to fulfill that purpose)?

In the first 11 chapters of Genesis, God's original intention and purpose for humanity dramatically unfolds. But before we look at these chapters it will be helpful to ponder briefly where the wider creation fits into this grand story. Why did God create *it* in the first place? Did he create this material universe simply because he needed a fitting arena to carry out his purposes *for us*? Many Christians have suggested that this is the case. But why, then, would God desire to save *this* creation, and to live within it for eternity?

If it were simply that we will need a place in which to live our future bodily existence, then God could easily replace this broken creation with a perfect and glorious one made solely of heavenly materials. Surely this would have been the way to do it. After all, wouldn't a heaven designed exclusively by God and built with pure heavenly materials (untouched by human hands) be much better than one constructed using earthly materials, including those feeble and finite contributions brought about by our work? Wouldn't a new, replacement heaven be better than a refurbished version of the creation that we, through our efforts, both shaped (to a large degree), and indeed broke?

As consummate consumers we know that a replacement, preferably a new model of the latest design, is always better than a reconditioned older model with refurbished and substandard parts. Or is it?

This wouldn't square with the story of salvation we have been exploring, however. God's desire to save this creation runs counter to, and goes much deeper than, the mindset of consumer culture. Genesis 1 – 11 suggests that there is a more profound reason why God has promised to recreate this natural universe rather than replace it.

Some Christians believe that it isn't appropriate to seek a *reason* for creation and salvation. God needs no other purpose than his decision to create and save, they say. While in an absolute sense this might be correct, if this is the *only* answer it doesn't help us at all. We are not questioning the purpose of existence in order to speculate impiously and beyond our station into the divine mysteries. Nor are we cynically testing God to see if his purposes are consistent. Rather, we are asking these questions so that we can know how to live accordingly. We want to understand these things, as far as we can, so that within God's purpose for us and for creation we can find our unique place and meaning. If God has a purpose for creating and saving us beyond the fact that he wants to, then knowing that purpose will enable us, through the Spirit, to re-envision, redirect, and integrate our own life stories into God's bigger creative story. Surely this is a genuine reason for doing theology. It's faith seeking to understand God's purpose for us and the rest of creation so that we can live godly lives accordingly.

A Play about Work: An Interactive Drama (Genesis 1 – 11)

So that we can interpret the stories of our own lives and see how each one might be grafted seamlessly into the narrative of God's creative purposes, we will go to the very beginnings of everything, to the opening chapters of the book of Genesis. Here, we find a story that suggests both why God created us within this world and what he is saving us for.

So how should we approach these somewhat tricky chapters? Because of its literary style, this text can seem quite peculiar to contemporary readers. Yet scholars suggest that these chapters "set the stage" for the rest of the book of Genesis and, in doing this, they also provide the plot and trajectory for what follows in the rest of the Bible. These chapters are, therefore, extremely important theologically, and learning to read them appropriately is vital.

According to their own shape and design, these chapters make the most sense if they are approached as a drama or a play of sorts. Some scholars even suggest that these chapters might have been crafted first and foremost to be acted out within the context of corporate Temple worship, and that Temple architecture itself might have reflected some of their structure.[15] This

[15] See, e.g., J. Richard Middleton, *The Liberating Image: The "Imago Dei" in Genesis 1* (Grand Rapids: Brazos Press, 2005), 81–88.

would mean, for example, that the shape of the text that we have was intended to be a type of script for the whole community to enact or dramatize in corporate worship. It's possible that it was designed to be sung responsively, so that through their active participation everyone present would see and feel themselves as a part of God's very act of creation from the beginning.

By beginning with God's creation of everything, and traveling through time right up to Abraham in chapter 12, the children of Abraham would, through worship, have come to comprehend their real identities and purpose in life. Those who felt themselves to be small, and who were continually oppressed and marginalized by the great nations around them, would have come to see themselves as significant and part of God's unfolding purposes for creation. The enactment of this drama would have allowed them to replace the virtual reality projected to them by the world with reality. They were God's people at the center of God's creative purposes.

Building upon this understanding of the text's possible original purpose, and guided as well by specific clues found within the text that we will see, we approach Genesis 1 – 11 something like what today we might call an interactive drama.

Yet in calling this text a drama we are not classifying the literary form of Genesis 1 – 11 as myth, as teaching religious or philosophical truth with pictures not corresponding to actual events. The inspired text itself suggests that the dramatizations are interpretations and adaptations, for the text's own theological purposes, of real happenings.

However, the text does not present these dramatizations simplistically, as transcriptions of what today we would call either historical or scientific processes. It is not as if a video camera perched at some objective vantage point recorded the events that the text describes. This text is simply not ordered or presented to us like that.

In either case, we are not focusing here on the actuality or otherwise of the events behind this narrative. Rather, for our purposes it is essential to let the text speak in its own way and on its own terms. Our goal is to catch the theology that flows from it. When we can see the coherent story that this text tells as the starting point for our Christian understanding of salvation, it will reshape our identities and sense of purpose in life. We now enter into the drama as the story invites us.

The Stage, the Players and the Acts (Genesis 1:1 – 2:3)

One of the first things that people notice about the creation story in Genesis is that there are actually two accounts. In the version of the story that we encounter first, from Genesis 1:1 – 2:3, God creates humankind following the creation of all other things. Genesis 2:4 – 5:1 then indicates that humanity's creation was first, directly after the creation of earth and the heavens. These two rather different versions of the story have caused many people, following a more modernist approach, problems over the years. Once we see how the first version of the story functions uniquely in relation to what follows, however, what for some has been a problem becomes a key to understanding the whole text on its own terms, as a drama.

One of my favorite films is the version of Shakespeare's *Henry* V starring Kenneth Branagh. It opens in darkness, and a narrator shatters the silence verbally (and visually by lighting a match), setting the stage for us and introducing the main theme and characters. This bit of off-stage monologue (which is actually on stage) lures the audience into the very heart of the story – it makes us a part of the story and the story a part of us. No matter how many times I see the film, the effect is the same – breathtaking and enveloping.

Once while watching this film it crossed my mind that maybe the Genesis 1 creation story functions in a similar way. It too begins abruptly and somewhat off-stage (at least in comparison with what we find in Genesis 2). It too draws us into the story by the way it sets the stage and introduces the main theme and players in the subsequent drama – a story that is in fact our story.

Is this, though, a fair way to understand the text? Somewhat to my surprise, I found upon further investigation that indeed it is.

While the creation account beginning in chapter 2 recounts a gradual and unfolding story complete with processes, detail and pace, chapter 1 begins literarily with a "big bang." Out of nothing and silence explode a flurry of images and creative activity. The specifics are given succinctly and in rapid succession. Chapter 1 begins by boldly declaring that in the beginning God created everything that exists, the heavens and the earth. Verses 3, 6, 9, 11, 14, 20, 24 and 26 then dramatically trumpet the formula "And God said . . ." and it was so, thereby setting the scene and introducing the main characters.

God himself is an actor, the main actor, but he is not placed upon the stage as the other actors are. Rather, the narrator sets God somewhat above the stage. Although God's actions make the drama possible and carry the plot along, there is a distinction between God and everything else in the story.

In the creation story beginning in chapter 2, by contrast, God interacts within and alongside, rather than above, the drama. The language, style, and tone of this account change completely and the narrative that carries us through to Abram at the end of chapter 11, and indeed beyond to the very end of the book, feels completely different. A paced rhythm, marked by the key phrase "This is the account (or generations) of . . ." replaces the bold explosion.

Although some translations fail to make clear its repetition, this catchphrase separates the acts in this drama. It functions like "Act 1" and "Act 2" notations in modern dramas. This verbal trigger (found in 2:4; 5:1, 6:9; 10:1; 11:10, 27; 25:12, 19; 36:1; 37:2) alerts us to the fact that the scene is changing and the story is moving on.

Genesis 1, however, reads completely differently from this rhythmic story told "generation by generation." These different styles are important, for they help us to discern the main themes of the overall drama.

The main theme in chapter 1 might at first seem difficult to discern because there is a double, or layered, theme. On one layer, the subject matter clearly is God the creator, the actor above the stage who sets the scene and remains distinct. On the next layer, the subject matter is also the creation itself. The narrative snappily arranges the set on the stage, bringing the entire act to a crescendo that in fact announces the other dimension of our double theme. This climax is none other than the creation of humanity beginning in verse 26.[16]

How does the text make this climax clear? From the beginning, and at each successive stage of creation in chapter 1, "Let there be . . ." functions as a trigger. Then, following the creation of some reality God pauses, but only briefly, to reflect on what he has done. To indicate its completion he then declares it to be "good."

With the creation of humankind, however, the language subtly shifts from "And God said, 'Let there be . . .' " to "And God said, 'Let us make man.' " This shift indicates that something unique is about to happen. God's pattern had been to make a declaration and then immediately create. With the creation of humanity, this pattern changes. Most noticeably God pauses after the initial declaration to offer a further rationale dramatizing the importance and purpose of what he is about to do. "Then God said, 'Let us make man in our image, in our likeness, and let them rule over the fish of the sea and the birds of the air . . .' " (v. 26). Then, following the creative act itself, the

[16] In order to correct the modern tendency of humanity to act as detached dominators of the natural order many contemporary commentators suggest that God's Sabbath, rather than the creation of humankind, is the climax of the story. Although equally concerned to challenge this notion that we can do whatever we want with the natural environment, as I will continue to explain, the text itself places humanity's creation at the climax.

narrative continues at this high pitch and intensity, explaining yet further God's commission to humanity to steward this creation. The climax comes with God's announcement that what he has made here is not just good, it is "very good" (v. 31).

The narrative, of course, does not end here. It continues on to open, as an umbrella covering everything, a different kind of day – the seventh day of rest, or Sabbath. Here the very language itself becomes more tranquil, as if to illustrate that the crescendo has passed and to communicate the meaning of the Sabbath itself. "Thus the heavens and the earth were completed in all their vast array. By the seventh day God had finished the work he had been doing; so on the seventh day he rested from all his work" (Gen. 2:1–2).

The very structure of this narrative emphasizes that humans, in their activity (work), and not only God in his work, will be the theme of the drama. We will be able to state this theme more succinctly when we turn to chapter 2, but first there are important details in chapter 1 that we need to observe – to develop our understanding of human purpose as well as our view of the place of human work within God's creative purposes.

From the Beginning: What on Earth Am I Doing?

There is more theology in Genesis chapter 1 than we can reflect upon here. We will focus, therefore, on several key points that will equip us to understand the story to follow, answer our questions why and for what purpose God made us, and ultimately build a theological view of work that works.

First, this account never questions that the material creation is good, and that it is therefore *in itself* valued by God. There is no hint that the material is simply a prison or "holding pattern" for a more real, but hidden, spiritual reality. Nor do we find any hint of the superiority of spirit over matter, spiritual over material, or sacred over secular. While persons are ordered over things, as we will see in a moment this is different from the ordering of persons over things presented in western theology (and criticized in Part I), where the internal (soul) is valued over physical reality. Indeed this account mentions neither the soul nor the creation of a distinctly "spiritual" realm (besides the reference to God's Spirit in v. 2).

The other important truths we will focus on in this creation account involve the creation of humanity. The first thing to notice here is that humankind is connected with, and similar to, the rest of the material creation. While, as we have seen, humanity is distinguished from the rest of creation in order to establish the theme, this is not the only dynamic within the text. Humanity is also set within creation, in a dependent relationship to it, and alongside God's other creatures.

When God creates the sea creatures and birds, he blesses them and also charges them to "Be fruitful and increase in number and fill the water . . . and the earth" (v. 22). This is the same phrase God uses to commission humanity after he creates them (v. 28). (There is, of course, a slight difference relating to humanity's unique purpose that we will explore in a moment.)

The point here is that to view humanity as *essentially* different from the rest of the material creation is a mistake. As we saw when we looked at the New Testament in Chapter 3, humans are natural beings, organically linked to the rest of creation such that even our salvation is the salvation of nature. It is not that God created nature simply to have a place to put us. Nor, as some Christians imply, was the physical body created to be a container to hold the "real us," or what they would think of as our souls.

God created us as real beings, with a spiritually physical existence. If God loves us, he loves nature. When God saves nature (and all that we have done through our work that subsequently becomes a part of creation), then, he is simply saving us fully. Were God not to save nature, including our work, then he would not be saving us as we really are.

This essential bond between nature and humanity (and our work as integral to who we are) is nowhere more clearly expressed than in the creation of humanity in God's image and likeness in Genesis 1:26–31. In verse 26 we see that God created humanity, male and female, in order to reflect God's very being. As we saw in the New Testament, the idea of humanity (later in the drama called Adam) being in God's image is the key to understanding Christ's work of salvation. Christ is the fulfillment of the image (the last Adam); we likewise "in Christ" become participants in the completed image (what Adam was intended to be). But what in the first place does it mean for humanity to have been created in God's image? And what was humankind intended originally to be?

According to this text there are at least two unavoidable dimensions to the answer. One is the essence of the image itself, and the other is the way that this nature is expressed. First, the essence of imaging God involves people together – and not merely a single person. No person, as an individual, can really reflect God's image. It is only in community (including both male and female) that we can adequately reflect God's nature.

Jesus, of course, is physically a single person. Theologically speaking, however, he is not. As the second person of the Trinitarian being of God, he is interdependent rather than independent. But even in his humanity he is, as we have seen, the head of the body. And that believers exist "in Christ" shows that he is something other than an individual in our sense of the word.

Thus, to be in God's image humanity must be in interdependent and co-operative relationships. The whole notion of an independent person, which is what modern society tries relentlessly to create, runs counter to what it means to be human in God's image and likeness. Nor, of course, does the notion of an independent person make any sense given the kind of oversight of creation required to adequately reflect God's image.

God's image is expressed through interdependence (see v. 26 and vv. 28–30). Expressing God's image means humanity, male and female, working throughout the material creation. It also involves, along with other creatures, our echoing back to God reflections of his nature through our pro-creative activity.

Yet humanity's primary *purpose* for existing, to image God, involves even more than this. It means going a step further by taking active responsibility for creation and shaping and reshaping it appropriately (ruling and subduing it) through our productive working activities. This does not mean that we find our purpose or identities through what we do in our work *apart* from our relationship with God. But nor, as some expressions of spirituality suggest, do we find our identities in some existential (touchy-feely) relationship with God alone, as if it were possible to image him apart from acting like him through our purpose, which is to work.

The "image of God" verses in Genesis 1 show us that our ordinary human work is an essential aspect of deepening our relationship with God – what today we might call being transformed into his image. Our relationship with God, our imaging him, is our essence as humans – while the working activity is the expression and realization of that essence.

If this is our human purpose, and salvation "in Christ" includes our being completed or fulfilled as that image, then our salvation itself means being set free "in Christ" to carry out our purpose – ordinary work. Salvation frees us to actually get on with work, but with the kind of godly work that some today have called "earth keeping."

We are, however, getting ahead of ourselves here. Although this theology is fully contained in Genesis chapter 1, the vision becomes even clearer as the drama unfolds from chapter 2. Even now we can see that this prologue to the drama, just like the narration beginning *Henry V*, draws us in and makes this story our story. But, as we know, what is coming is not all good news.

Promising Failures: God's Image Bearers at Work

To plot the story of our lives within the larger biblical story of human destiny requires that we know where we were headed to begin with and what happened to us along the way. We can see this clearly in the following sketch of the drama in Genesis 2–11.

This overview, including a few more in-depth analyses of acts most relevant to our questions, is no substitute for carefully reading and listening to the entire drama. A drama is primarily to be experienced, not summarized and analyzed. Our focus here in following this interpretation is to highlight some of the details that are often overlooked.

As we begin, we look in the text for clues that will help us to name the main theme, or title, of the play. We know from Genesis 1 that God in his work as creator, as well as humanity in our work commissioned to mirror him, are both at the heart of the story. Indeed, this mandate to image God, expressed through our co-operative work with God, weaves together each of the important theological details in our plot.

So what is this drama about? As we have seen, the phrase "these are the generations of" provides our first clue. This strategic marker indicates that our story is in fact about human beings and the unfolding of human culture using, and within, the material creation. Throughout the drama are people, linked to each other as family, who are portrayed as either appropriately or hideously imaging God in the physical world. As they give creation its tangible shape, they create early world history.

Yet this doesn't mean, as modern society would have us believe, that humans alone create and shape reality. In this drama God is intimately and actively involved. Not only does he alone provide the raw material and appropriate conditions. He also, without directly scripting it, keeps the drama moving – as he interacts with, responds to, and even prods his creation toward the gracious purposes he has for it. We repeatedly (though not always) resist his involvement, and at these points God stiffens his resolve and tactics. He simply loves creation too much to be pushed out of the picture and leave us to our own devices.

The drama shows these two genuinely creative agents at work. Humans are depicted as co-workers with God.

Admittedly, this partnership is uneven. God is clearly the senior, or master, in the relationship. God makes our creative working possible in the first place. He uses whatever we do to direct us toward his purposes, which always means toward our flourishing as created beings.

The drama does, of course, require us to adlib in our parts along the way. While we are given the mandate, the script allows us as actors to use the stage and the props we are given as we want.

So how might we summarize the theme? We could say that this drama presents the actions of humanity, sometimes in a right relationship with God but often not, carrying out our responsibility as shapers of the earth. This seems to capture the dynamic of the "tragedy" so that the title could be "Promising Failures: God's Image Bearers at Work."

The Curtain Rises: Act 1, Scene 1

The story itself begins in Genesis 2:4 with the account, or "genealogy," of the earth and the heavens. Verses 4–5 announce that God at first kept the earth lifeless and empty precisely because there was not yet anybody "to work the ground."

So, to get things moving, in verses 6 and 7 God waters the dry ground. From that moistened dust he creates, first of all, Adam. With this order of creation God places humanity center stage. Adam, made from the stuff he will be commissioned to work on, is God's appointed worker. The inference here is fascinating: when Adam works on nature, he is also working on himself. Adam's very being, future, and identity are bound up with the earth and his work upon it. His future is thus nature's future, and vice versa. Likewise, we must also say that work's future is his future, and vice versa. As we will soon see, Adam will need to be restored (saved) in order for him to have any real future. But this restoration of his life and identity will require the restoration of the earth. And the earth here includes what Adam does to himself, as well as to the earth, through his work.

To exclude from salvation either of these dimensions would ultimately be to save something other than the actual Adam.

All life on earth is bound up with, and indeed seems to flow from, Adam. In verse 7 God gives life to the creation by first breathing life into this *earthy* creation – Adam. And only after Adam becomes a living being does God bring the rest of creation to life. Creation's life is a gift from God – and God links this life-full creation inextricably with Adam's.

In verse 8 we see that God fleshes out and orders creation by planting a garden. He puts Adam in the middle of it, surrounding him with life and everything he needs for life. This is no drab existence but plentiful, proportioned, and beautiful. The setting is perfect not in the sense of being finished, for work needed to be done, but in the sense that everything is there and ready. Well, almost everything.

Before God ever gives any "forbidding" command, he places Adam in the garden for the purpose of working it – in a caring manner, reflecting the way God himself had created everything (v. 15). It is only after placing him here and after giving Adam the freedom to gather food from all other trees that, in verse 16, God tells Adam not to eat from the tree of the knowledge of good and evil. For Adam to fulfill his commission appropriately, his food-gathering "work" must bypass this one tree.

The text in no way suggests that God, by introducing this prohibition, is being sadistic or that he is teasing or tempting Adam. Perhaps God is showing Adam that some things are for God alone – after all, Adam is just the apprentice. Or maybe Adam was not yet ready for what this tree had to offer. While the story does not state the purpose of this tree or the prohibition, it is clear that for God's project to work for the good of Adam, and creation, Adam must go about his work in God's way.

And so he does – at first. Verse 18 reiterates what we saw in Genesis 1. For our good, God designed that we should not work as isolated individuals. For Adam's work to be fulfilling, he needs a partner to work at his side. God gently brings Adam himself to this realization by creating other living creatures and setting Adam to work naming them. In fulfilling this task Adam reveals his potential as God's image bearer by not only recognizing the distinctions (order) that God has built into nature, but also by adding to creation names or identities that previously did not exist. This is co-operation between God and Adam at its finest. Adam is giving shape to creation in a way that respects both its integrity and its diversity.

In the course of this work, Adam realizes that he has not yet found a suitable helper. At this point, God steps in and works on his behalf. In verses 21–22 God forms Adam's counterpart – from Adam, but according to God's own design. He then offers her to Adam. Adam is pleased and, as part of working upon himself, this further "dust of the earth" (only this time taken from his own self), Adam names her "woman."

In no way does this text suggest that Adam is either superior to her or supposed to rule her. She is a part of him, like nature but even more so, for she is his very "flesh and bones." Human identity includes our relationship with nature and work, but it also includes, most intimately, our relationship with other humans. Adam is simply not complete without another beside him. Although this specifically implies the husband-wife relationship, it also includes the breadth of our social relationships. For it simply is not good for someone to be, and work, completely alone.

Man and woman were thus off to a good start imaging God their creator. Their work as apprentices was well underway. But this was not to last long. Beginning in Genesis 3 and continuing through Genesis 4, we find what is commonly referred to as the Fall of humanity and of creation.

Most of us know the events of Genesis 3 well. Possibly while man and woman are working on their different tasks (assuming they were going about the garden fulfilling their God-given purpose), the serpent approaches the woman and deceives her. She decides to take food, and eat, from the forbidden tree.

As suggested, maybe God had his own plan and own time for bringing humanity to a place of maturity where he could give them the "knowledge of good and evil." Maybe God himself was planning to feed them from this tree one day, but not before they were ready. Maybe God never intended them to have this food and knowledge. Again, the story is silent on this matter and leaves us to wonder.

We do know that, when woman eats and then gives the food to her husband and he eats, this act of disobedience reveals humanity trying to skirt around what God knows to be the best way for them to work and live. They choose to express their identities by doing their God-given work (gathering and eating fruit from the trees) autonomously and apart from God. Maybe they were trying to reach their final destiny in their own way by taking a short cut.[17] Maybe they did not yet know that such "godlikeness" or maturity was to be their destiny, but only that such a thing sounded good at the time. Either way, disaster results when we try to image God and achieve our destiny in our own way. When we try to work ignoring God, we actually distort God's image.

Beginning in Genesis 3:7 we notice that the harmonious relationship between humans, Adam and his wife, is broken. Also, as a part of this same reality (vv. 7–13), we see that humanity's unimpeded (though not yet continual) relationship with God is broken.

From verse 14 we see the long-range consequences of trying to achieve God's purposes for ourselves in our own way. First, God curses the serpent, the tempter, and declares hostility between this animal and humanity (although in v. 15 God does allude to the promise that this will one day be overcome). Then in verse 16 God turns to humanity, his centerpiece in

---

[17] We can see clear parallels between this incident and Satan in the wilderness tempting Jesus to bow down to him and receive through a short cut what we know to be his destiny (Matt. 4:8–10).

creation. The work of woman, he says, carrying out her specific God-imaging function through childbirth (the multiplication and filling the earth aspect of the commission), will involve pain. Likewise, her broken relationship with Adam will mean that he will now rule over her.

Presumably Adam would have felt the sting of this latter curse too, as his interdependent relationship with his sexual and working partner, his friend, becomes twisted. Yet this is not all Adam has to face. The ground, nature, the very stuff from which he himself is made, is cursed. And thus his own identity is unimaginably torn apart. And as he is alienated from the ground, he is alienated from himself. Further, new and ambivalent life will emerge from the earth and will present to Adam all sorts of frustrating problems that he will experience most directly in his work. Work is cursed, and in order to survive he will have to endure painful "sweat and toil" (vv. 17–19). Ultimately, life itself will be taken from him. Thus Adam, who was but dust to begin with, will return lifeless to the dusty ground.

Once back to work, somewhat ironically, Adam "named his wife Eve, because she would become the mother of all the living" (v. 20). God's commission to multiply and work the earth has neither ceased nor been suspended. His purpose and grace for humanity has not ended. Yet how ironic and tragic that from Adam and Eve will come all the "living," now characterized by death and decay.

Lest in this condition they eat from the tree of life, God has to banish humanity from the garden. While our purpose is still to work the ground, now (until the new creation) we find ourselves in wilderness conditions, with no recourse to the tree of life (vv. 22–24).

Genesis 4 demonstrates the nature of our Fall in a parallel way. The alienated relationship between brothers Cain and Abel, resulting in Cain murdering Abel, reflects the enmity between all children of humanity. As this story begins, Abel is at work in animal husbandry and Cain in horticulture (v. 2).

Things quickly go awry in their relationships with each other and in Cain's relationship with God. Cain takes Abel to the field (v. 8), his workplace, and kills him – possibly using the very tools and technology that he invented and had been using for proper godly ends.

Appropriately, Cain's curse for killing his brother is likewise directly related to his daily work (vv. 11–14). He is alienated from the ground (his own nature) and his very way of being, which is his work. His identity is taken away from him and so, by his act, he becomes dehumanized. The result is that he becomes, by his own fault, an unsettled wanderer or refugee. But still he is not beyond God's grace (vv. 15–16). God's purposes for humanity, even Cain, continue.

Many of the good things in human culture are said to come even from Cain and his descendents. Human inventions including cities (v. 17), textile work and developments in animal husbandry (v. 20), the arts or music making (v. 21), and various kinds of metallurgy and tool manufacture (v. 22) all continue apace. Human culture, through its work, continues to unfold and indeed things even start to look up, as humans again "began to call upon the name of the Lord" (v. 26).

The beginning of Genesis 5 signals the next scene change. We travel through time up to Noah and the drama of the flood. Humans have become so corrupt and violent while spreading out, ruling, and subduing the earth that, apart from Noah and his family, God has to clean the stage and start all over again.

God gives a special work commission to Noah, to build an ark. And, as a type of the real Adam, Noah takes the animal creation with him to safety and salvation. Noah and his family, alone among all the people, image God properly, according to our commission.

After the flood, God explicitly re-establishes with Noah his commission to humankind, begun anew, to be God's very image. Our purpose is to keep spreading out and increasing (9:6–7).

This is exactly what happens, even through Noah's youngest son Ham in the family winery business, until he then blows it.

But, even then, human beings get back on track. Throughout Genesis 10 human cultures continue, as God intends, to expand and disperse. Each develops its own political systems and languages (vv. 5, 20, 31).

Yet in Genesis 11 trouble resurfaces. In the midst of carrying out its God-imaging purposes, humanity once again squanders its potential. It attempts to carry out its commission in its own twisted way.

Genesis 11:2–4 clearly explain the rationale behind God's choice to scatter the nations and confuse their languages. In verse 6 the Lord says, "If as one people speaking the same language they have begun to do this, then nothing they plan to do will be impossible for them." Why should this worry God? Surely we are no threat to him? Our tower couldn't even reach heaven. He had to come down to even see the city (v. 5).

As always, God's concern was for our sakes. The details revealing how God saw the problem and its potential for harm are illuminating. In verse 2, humanity is spreading out and moving eastward – apparently according to God's "fill the earth" commission to Adam and Noah. But verses 3 and 4 bring us to an abrupt halt. For people have decided to use work – building technology, in particular – to thwart God's purposes. Humanity's pride has gotten the better of them as they plan to build upward, to reach God themselves, rather than building outward as God had instructed. They chose to stop and build precisely so that they would no longer have to spread out across the face of the earth (v. 4). People were still working, developing technology, and building – but in contradiction to God's larger purposes (what today we might call his kingdom purposes). They wanted to work, but not as co-workers with God.

God's statement in verse 6, then, makes sense. If he allows people to do this they will, through vile pride and ultimately by veering from God's gracious and wise purposes for them, be hurting only themselves. So what did God do? He had to stop them, and so he did (vv. 7–8).

God's judgement in confusing the languages ensured that humanity would get back on track and continue to fill the whole earth. Of course now, rather than spreading out freely under our own initiative, we are scattered (v. 9). God is not to be trifled with. But, even here, we see God's grace in action. For what he did in this judgement was to direct us back to his good purposes for us. As in Genesis 10, people soon got back to work and to developing those things through work, like societies and languages, that are not all bad. Indeed, in the new creation these things will be a part of the "glory" that we bring to the new city.

Finally a Theology that Works

The drama we have witnessed is quite remarkable, as is the theology it teaches about creation, our lives, and our work. As we bring Part II to a close, we summarize here the main points of this story. Each of the following points carries from the Old Testament into the New, and each is an important ingredient in our answers to questions about work. Each point will also help us to finish building our new view of work in the next two chapters.

Humans in ordinary work are God's apprentices, his co-workers. Contrary to the myths of modern culture that tell us progress and happiness result from being a self-made man or woman according to our production and consumption of goods, humans do not create themselves through work. God created humanity, and so ultimately our existence and welfare depend upon him. The responsibility and pressure to invent ourselves through our technology and achievements are, as history has shown us, indeed more than we can bear. This does not diminish the fact, however, that we have a God-given mandate to extensively shape and reshape the world through our work. As we do this, of course, we shape ourselves time and again – and ultimately we shape the future as well. Yet, we never work alone. Even when we try to do it without him, God is always there working as well. Sometimes God remains in the background – responding, fixing, prodding. Sometimes he is in the foreground, working out his own purposes directly and ahead of us. Ordinary work in this world is a joint project between the master and his apprentices.

Central as it is, work is not all there is to this life. Although this book focuses on the centrality and value of daily work within God's purposes, clearly work is not the be all and end all of life. Work, both for God and for us, has its limits. Although work is essential and is in one form or another the context for so much that takes place in our lives, the final word both for God and for us is the Sabbath. An existence without rest and space to reflect on our lives – what we have done, what we are doing, who we are and who we are becoming – is no existence at all. As we will see in Chapter 5, however, Sabbath does not always mean inactivity. It reflects, rather, a rhythm and quality of life that at times simply let humanity and the world be.

Imaging God physically is our destiny and identity as humans. God created physical things because they are different from him. What may seem an obvious point, therefore, is not *always* quite so obvious in our living – we don't need to feel guilty that we are not God. We are not finite, limited, peculiar, and a "work in progress" as a result of the Fall, nor are these qualities a hindrance to living. God created us to flourish – but as human and natural beings. Salvation does not deliver us from this; it gives us the freedom to get back to our purpose and to be the "secular" workers God intended us to be.

Likewise, although God could have created both humans and the world as finished products, he didn't. God created us complete, fully equipped to fulfill our purpose. But he didn't create us "perfect" in the sense of being finished. We cannot understand who we are at the deepest level, and our right place in this world, apart from this. God created us for the process as well as the goal. And this process includes our work upon the creation. It appears that God's purpose was always to live right next to creatures who are genuinely "other," who are distinct from him yet whose very way of life significantly reflects his own by being relational, harmonious, creative, and productive. It also follows that he always wanted to live with and within a living natural environment, which would be brought to maturity both by him and by his apprentices. This is a world with room for the Fall – but it does not require it.

We work now in a world that is not yet redeemed. As glorious and purposeful as work is, we must remember that, since the Fall and under the conditions of the curse, our work and what it produces are ambivalent at best. Even the most enjoyable, meaningful, and humanly important work includes aspects of toil and frustration. Even when our motives are right and we work for God's glory and to benefit others, our best achievements and products will be characterized significantly by decay. And what we build for good, others can and often do use for death and evil. Technology is a wonderful and a horrible thing. Our earth keeping has led to some wonderful achievements for both humanity and nature, but in the process we have also often contributed to destruction among ourselves and in our environment.

We work now in a world that is already redeemed. Frustration and decay are not the whole picture, however. We don't live in a world that is only fallen. We live somewhat like Christ did between the resurrection and ascension – in between worlds. Though not yet fully, this world and those in it who are "in Christ" have already been restored and set free to be ourselves and to flourish – through the life, death, and resurrection of Christ. In the Spirit we do have the potential, to some degree at least, to anticipate the new creation, to bring about within this creation states of affairs that anticipate the future glorification of ourselves, of nature, and of our work. We can imagine ourselves doing it differently from Adam and Eve, Cain, and the others. And we can enact these possibilities in our work as well as in other areas of life. Indeed, this is what it means in this life to glorify God and live according to our purpose.

PART III

Heavenly Minded *and* Good for the Earth

Work, Spirituality and Mission

5

Justifying our Work: A Spirituality of Work that Works

For it is by grace you have been saved, through faith – and this not from yourselves, it is the gift of God – not by works, so that no-one can boast.
Ephesians 2:8–9

The spiritual man makes judgements about all things.
1 Corinthians 2:15

In Part I, we cleared the ground and laid the foundation for developing a theologically robust understanding of work that fully and equally integrates our spiritual and physical lives and thus offers hope to Christians who devote so much of themselves to ordinary work. In Part II, we reflected theologically on a number of biblical passages in order to better understand why Christians can, and indeed should, believe in "the heavenly good of earthly work."

Now, in these final two chapters, we will build upon all of this to explore how ordinary working believers can live "first-class" Christian lives, full of both meaning and purpose. We will explore some of what it means to be spiritually liberated rather than frustrated in our work. Being "heavenly minded" in this way can be good for this earth (people and nature) and also good for the future earth to come.

In this chapter we will define the contours of a spirituality of work that is liberating for Christians at work. In the final chapter, then, we will re-think what this means for the direction and practice of Christian mission. Why and how is mission what the whole people of God *are* about while at work, whether consciously or not? And why and how does mission entail our work itself?

Understandably some might be concerned that this revised understanding of spirituality and mission could lead to believers neglecting the importance of evangelism, of sharing our hope and telling the Christian story to others outside the faith and inviting them to join us. Yet nothing that we have seen so far would suggest that this would follow. Nor will it result from what we offer here.

On the contrary, although this concern is genuine, what follows from the theology we have seen and our reflections here on spirituality and mission is a way to express our hope for salvation that most of us can share quite naturally. This is because our hope is integral to who we are and what we do when we work – not just when we're at church. This hope, at the core of who we are and not just in some "religious" part of our life, is a vision of salvation that most people in the workplace would find compelling – our life and our faith integrated.

Allowing this hope to transform how we go about our ordinary working lives is, by and large, what I mean by a spirituality of work. This includes our being a specific kind of "spiritual" person at work and embodying a spirituality as described below. At this point, a word is in order about the language we use to talk about this integration of the ordinary and the spiritual. So far, the theology that we have seen shows that we must stop thinking of the "physical" (and thus ordinary work) and the "spiritual" as distinct, as two separate spheres or kingdoms. Yet it is almost impossible to avoid using both of these words, or categories, altogether. In this life heaven and earth have not yet been fully united – at least not as they will be in the new creation. So what can we do? Armed with our new theology, the task is to redefine, or conceptualize afresh, what we usually mean by the word "spiritual." We will do this most effectively if we understand "spiritual" to be about God's value of, and goal for, the "physical" creation. But it also involves grasping that the ordinary work we do is *itself* spiritual and transforming – and therefore missional.

Salvation with Work, not by Work(s)

In societies influenced by western values and ways of working, the temptation is immense to try to create ourselves and justify our existence through our work. The spirituality that emerges from the theology we have been exploring runs counter to this kind of salvation through work(s). In fact, it undermines any work(s) salvation that might threaten to creep in the back door to destroy us.

To believe that our work will be saved along with us (because it is a part of nature and of our identity) is not the same as believing that we can or will be saved by, through, or because of our work(s). Luther was quite right to insist that all Christian living should flow from the justification that God alone provides. This is because Christ's atoning work is all that is needed to justify our existence. And, if we don't approach our life and work with the belief that our existence has already been justified by God, then it will be extremely hard to avoid the temptation of trying to justify ourselves by what we do and accomplish.

Whether or not we follow Luther's method for understanding specifically how justification reorients Christian spirituality and ethics (his earthly and heavenly kingdoms approach), one thing is certain. We will only have the spiritual freedom we need to engage meaningfully in any of life's activities, including our daily work, if we know that we no longer have to try to invent ourselves, and then make ourselves acceptable through them, either to God or others. The starting point for a spirituality of work is the security of knowing that God in Christ accepts us as we are – and that therefore we don't have to justify ourselves to anyone – God or people.

Experiencing this freedom will, in turn, allow us to get beyond our obsessions with ourselves and allow us to give ourselves fully to our work and, through this, to others. Without being liberated from creating and recreating ourselves, we will constantly be trying to prove to ourselves, to God, and to others that we are worth loving – in spite of our inadequacies and even sin. Most of us know the crushing pressure and futility of trying to achieve self-worth and peace through work.

"So, what do you do?" is often the first question people ask us. This question is not wholly inappropriate since work is, by virtue of God's design, an aspect of our identities. Spiritually speaking, however, asking this question is only appropriate when we come at it having already experienced God's prior justification for our existence. Otherwise, the other person (and perhaps we ourselves) will measure our status and "worth" according to our professional standing. Only the liberty that comes by our justification lets us fathom what the real, even eternal, value of our work might be.

As Ephesians 2:8–10 suggests, it is only after we see that our works, religious or otherwise, can't save us that we become liberated for our destiny – which is to produce good works. As Luther said, justification frees us to genuinely love God and our neighbor.

So do our works accomplish anything "spiritually"? Certainly nothing we do pays God back for what he has done for us. If we could do this, then Christ's work on the cross would be simply an advance or loan, rather than the full payment that it is.

Nor do we justify through our work God's decision to justify us – as if through our productivity we could show God that he made a good choice when calling us. It is worrying that this is precisely what a lot of Protestant and evangelical spirituality inadvertently suggests. Indeed, our leaders often model this by engaging unceasingly in work/ministry activities. We seem to fall easily into this trap.

This sort of workaholic spirituality results from a missing, or bad, theology of work(s). Driven and workaholic Christians are, deep down, often hoping that their work(s) will pay God back (and thus relieve their sense of guilt).

The way we use songs, sermons, and prayers can also reveal some of these misguided beliefs. Sometimes, to convict and challenge ourselves to serve God more fully, we sing of offering to him "our life and our all." Yet we do not mean that our life and all is acceptable because of salvation, but rather that this salvation somehow "demands" it. We see offering "our life and our all," then, either as a way to pay God back for salvation, or as the way to justify God's calling us.

This subtly twisted and superficial understanding of justification destroys our spirituality. Because, rather than seeing our work(s) as our appropriate human way of life – a way that paradoxically once in Christ sets us free to live healthily by imaging God according to his purposes – we often skew the concept of Christian obedience into a kind of deal with God. If we really thought it through we would have to acknowledge that we can never pay God back for his gift – but still we keep trying. People today, unlike some of our Puritan ancestors, are less likely to see work as a way of gaining confidence that they are elected by God. However, many of us see our work(s) as the way we make things "even" between us and God.

A bad theology of work(s), therefore, leads to a failure to enter genuinely into our salvation/justification. There are complex reasons for this, but part of it is that our work(s) are a part of who we are, and they cannot help but seek some kind of spiritual home. If we don't find an appropriate spiritual category for our work, then it takes over our lives and becomes alien to us. It begins to dominate us as we become *dis*-integrated people.

As we have seen, our work finds its spiritual justification, its ultimate home and value, through our justification. Our work is an outworking and expression of who we are. Thus, our justification becomes our work's justification too. Through our freedom in Christ, our work(s) becomes set free so that it has a genuine earthly usefulness now, but also a continued existence, like we do, in heaven.

Our work does not save us, nor does it build God's kingdom for him. Only God can build his kingdom and bring about his new creation – whether in people, on earth now, or in the new heaven and the new earth. But justification does restore us to fulfill our original purpose – to be God's growing and ever more skillful co-workers.

Modern Work: Bringing Hell to Earth?

It is also important to see that our spirituality of work steers us well clear of modern beliefs claiming that human ingenuity alone can create heaven on earth. For example, rationalized labor and "advancing" technology were meant to free us from the need for religion by bringing a new kind of paradise to earth now. Yet this modern salvation has more often than not ended up creating hell instead for many people around the world, and for the environment.

When we do not seek the future in God, we end up looking for hope elsewhere – and our built-in human longings for a future, growth, and progress will compel us to try to create utopia for ourselves. This tendency to work toward some vision of heaven on earth shouldn't surprise us. Nor is the tendency wrong in itself. God designed our hearts this way. He created us to reflect him as his working apprentices within the material creation with a bent toward our future. But without God and his kingdom in focus, all of our visions of what this future should look like become misdirected and are bound to go wrong. And if theology alone were not enough to convince us, the last couple of centuries of world history prove that we are not very good at creating heaven without God through our work and technology.

According to modernist thinking, of course, "heaven" was a Christian myth. At best, the concept was a piece of religious irrelevance that we have replaced with the idea of inevitable human progress. At worst, moderns saw heaven as a harmful drug that deceived people into seeking a hope for a paradise beyond this life. The hope for heaven, then, numbed us into blindly accepting broken and oppressive realities rather than leading us to try to change them. The charge? That Christians were "so heavenly minded that they were of no earthly good."

Moderns, having decided that they could do a better job than God, abandoned the future heaven of faith. They relocated "heaven" to this life and proclaimed that it could be achieved here and now if we simply work hard enough. That is, they decided to save themselves by building heaven now – through work – Babel revisited. Whether this is the consumer-capitalist or communist version, the root belief is the same: *progress through hard work will save us.*

There is no denying that our work has produced some reasonable results. For example, the moderate success of modern democracy, scientific discovery, and various technologies that make life and the world better for some, are good things. However, these human wonders also have a dark side that has led to untold suffering for many millions. The pressure to create a Utopia now, through our work and without God, has become a weight far too heavy for us to bear.

This pressure to "make heaven" has caused the modern belief in inevitable "progress" to implode. World Wars I and II, the Cold War, and the current ecological crises are just some examples of the underbelly of modernity's efforts, through work, to bring about heaven on earth. Mechanized work, overwork, and workaholism are just a few of the problems that result from the compulsive drive to create what only God himself can create.

The problem is not the human desire for heaven. It is rather that we in the modern west (like the men and women in Genesis), through a misguided belief in what we can accomplish by ourselves without God, have destroyed at least as much as we have created. The tragic truth is that we have created new versions of hell rather than paradise.

The biblical theology and spirituality of work that we are exploring here stands in stark contrast to modernist thought. It begins with God's justification of our existence and the promise of a different kind of work. Since we don't have to accomplish *everything* in our co-working with God, we have space for non-work, or Sabbath – for rest and spiritual reflection on who we are and what we have done. Sabbath, rather than being the opposite of work, becomes the very thing that characterizes our work. For from rest and godly reflection comes genuinely humane work. When we are reflecting God appropriately, therefore, all of our work will be seasoned with Sabbath. And Sabbath living opens up creation itself so that creation becomes a genuine "living space" for us and for others.

This theology of work thus offers a life now and a future home for us and the earth that both, as well as God, can live with. The vision incorporates our transformed work but does not rely on it to bring us, or the world, to completion.

Therefore, rather than crumbling under the pressure to make something of our world, we are now free to let God create heaven for us. The fact that God in "making all things new" chooses to incorporate our work(s) motivates us but does not crush us. It fills our work with meaning and purpose – but not more than we as humans can bear. That God is ultimately responsible to bring about the new creation lightens our load. For only when our version of heaven gets out of the way does a space in our experience open up that allows God to put his version in its place. This confidence is what allows us to resist the hell of secular salvation.

This does not mean that we simply sit back and wait for heaven. Although our best efforts now are ambivalent at best, the good news is that God the master craftsman is responsible for finishing the work. Since it is not our job to make all things new, in our work we simply do our best to creatively reflect God and embody heavenly "kingdom values" in every sphere of life. Our work may, from time to time, even be somewhat successful, and thus bring joy and satisfaction – for the time being. But this is not the burden of having to be perfect. Our work(s) can be good without needing to be perfect since it is

God's work to perfect them ultimately. Even if at times we might prove to have been mistaken in our efforts, we know that even these efforts are not beyond God's healing touch and ultimate transformation into "his best work." For "we know that in all things God works for the good of those who love him, who have been called according to his purpose" (Rom. 8:28).

The secular salvation of modernist work creates hell instead of heaven because such work has to masquerade as something it can never be. It has to be faultless – and to be perfect without passing through God's discerning, redeeming, and purifying judgement is impossible.

Judgement Needed

Ultimately, for our work to reflect and thus glorify God, it needs to be rigorously judged. Our spirituality of work, however, incorporates judgement in more than the traditional "religious" sense of the word. Obviously all of our life and work will be judged by God in the end. Who we are, and whatever we "build," must go through God's judging fires (1 Cor. 3:9–15). Yet there is another sense of judgement that we as God's apprentices are called to exercise already regarding how we live and work. "The spiritual man makes judgements about all things" (1 Cor. 2:15).

First, then, we want to explore the meaning and purpose of God's judgement of his apprentices' works and lives. A spirituality that ignores this judgement cannot be Christian. God's prior judgement, of course, justified us and our work. Rather than undermining or denying this, God's further judgement defines and completes his initial justifying judgement.

What, then, will it mean for us to reflect God as we make regular judgements about what we do and how we do it? And how can this spirituality of work deepen our faith and walk with God beyond what our old view of work, or of spirituality, ever could?

The understanding of heaven and justification that we have been exploring leads to a particular understanding of what

God's judgement is and how he will carry it out. So the first question we need to address is this: What is the nature and purpose of God's judgement on all human activity, and the whole physical universe?

As we have seen, there are basically two ways to understand what God will do in judgement with this earth and everything in it. Either the new earth will be fundamentally dissimilar to this one, a pristine replacement, or it will be a healed and restored version of this one. According to the latter view, the new earth will be "resurrected," a fulfilled or perfected continuation of this one – although by virtue of its transformation through judgement it will be much more than this one ever could have been.

The first view, often called "annihilationist," sees God's judgement as primarily punitive. God's punishment of creation will lead to its total destruction and replacement with a new earth that God will make "out of nothing," as he did the original creation. 2 Peter 3:10–13 is often quoted as proof of this view that nothing from this life will endure. "But the day of the Lord will come like a thief. The heavens will disappear with a roar; the elements will be destroyed by fire, and the earth and everything in it will be laid bare . . . But in keeping with his promise we are looking forward to a new heaven and a new earth, the home of righteousness."

Those who hold this view do not, of course, contend that believing people will be replaced in this way. A believer's salvation preserves his or her life and guarantees that he or she will not be annihilated. Salvation applies only to people, however. God will replace everything else – all non-human life, all physical realities – with something like the Garden of Eden, pristine and unaffected by humanity.

This is not, however, the vision of the new creation that we've seen unfolding through Scripture. Nor is 2 Peter 3:10–13 best read in an annihilationist manner. Indeed the judgement it speaks of penetrates to the very elemental depth of material existence. It must. For this judgement needs to eliminate, or "destroy," all the sin that has permeated the fabric of creation that would prevent it becoming genuinely new. Although a few obscure Greek manuscripts suggest that "the earth and everything in it will be *burned up*," the most reliable Greek manuscripts suggest (as rendered in the NIV) that "the earth and everything in it will be *laid bare*." Thus, judgement then purges this earth and everything in it rather than replacing it.

Contrary to the annihilationist view is another, commonly called the transformational view, that emerges from and is consistent with our reflections on the resurrection of the body. The transformational view understands salvation to be cosmic in scope, flowing from the human Christ, through our resurrection to all that exists (Rom. 8:19–25). It sees God's judgement on the whole creation as ultimately healing, restoring it for eternal existence. Following the idea that God has justified us and our work, it understands God's judgement to be transformative as it brings to fullness his purposes for us and the rest of creation.

This understanding of judgement begins with seeing the goodness of material creation and its value to God. Of course, the sin and death that we bring to the creation threaten to completely destroy us and the creation, and this enrages God. Yet although sin and death have succeeded in alienating the entire creation from its joyful relationship with God for awhile, they have not completely destroyed the goodness or value of creation. God's judgement "in Christ" has already fallen, and finally will fall, on sin and all the death, decay, and loss that is bound up with and results from it. For the material creation has neither in itself nor due to sin ceased to be an object of God's love.

Yet, for this cleansing to happen, God's judgement *will* need to destroy all traces of sin and death, "far as the curse is found," as the hymn "Joy to the World" says. And sin's effects are everywhere deeply embedded in us. God, through the penetrating fire of judgement, will extract sin and its harmful effects, thereby purifying what remains.

Many of us are used to thinking about this kind of transformative judgement in relation to believers. Fewer of us would apply it to the whole cosmos. Fewer still, it seems, have realized that this judgement involves our work itself, which is now a part of this creation.

These reflections are not mere abstract speculations. To be consistent, God's judgement must square with his justification of creation and our lives. And how we understand justification and judgement together will determine what we think about the value of the natural world and of the things done on earth by humans.

To know every detail about heaven – the new creation – is ultimately beyond our grasp. Nor is such knowledge needed. Heaven is a mystery, and all attempts to literalistically describe our work's place therein, even if drawn from good and consistent theological thinking, will be at best only tentative. Our sanctified imaginations can only suggest what we think God's promise to make *all* things new might mean. Yet this is exactly the approach that writers of the biblical prophetic and apocalyptic texts took when, directed by the Spirit, they encouraged God's people to hang in there amidst life's frustrations. As this biblical literature suggests, only a theologically consistent and suggestive envisioning of our eternal destiny will give us the vision and motivation we need to live now according to God's kingdom values.

So what does all of this mean for our spirituality of work? That God will need to purify our work before he integrates it into the very fabric of the new creation sounds promising. But how does this help us now? The things we build eventually fall apart. We bake the cake to eat it, not to have it last forever. Most of the results of our work fade away immediately, or at least within our own lifetimes. How could we possibly see these results in God's final transformation of this earth?

Realities like these keep us from proposing too simplistic or too literalistic a view of our work's salvation or glorification. If God can raise and transform the dead, however, he can raise and transform all present and even past (decayed and gone) earthly realities.

Yet, rather than limiting our thinking to individual products of work, it may also help us to think about the cumulative nature and impact of our work on this earth and on the whole of humanity. Think about how different our world would be had someone not invented the wheel. God's judgement about the "goodness" or otherwise of the wheel we invented does not apply only to the "original" wheel. It involves a judgement of all that has resulted from there being wheels – all that we have built upon, and from, and with, this invention.

Today we live with the results, good and bad, of what previous generations did through their work. Every product of work, and every way of working, in some way preserves and develops what has come before. Human beings stand on one another's shoulders all the way back to Adam. Rather than thinking individualistically about the salvation of unrelated separate entities, it might help us to see our work interdependently as part of the "fabric of this world" (as Lee Hardy calls it[18]) that God will preserve and transform into the fabric of the new earth.

There will be, no doubt, some specific products of our work that through judgement will be transformed and incorporated into the "new physics" of the new creation. I am quite hoping that Handel's *Messiah* will be regularly in concert in the New Jerusalem. Likewise, it would sorely disappoint me now to think that I will not have eons to fly my paraglider and to sharpen and develop my skills and understanding of the new creation through this.

As we saw in Revelation 21 and 22, there is no reason why God's judgement would exclude some of the nobler objects of human culture from being integral parts of the new creation (transformed, of course, as we are seeing here, through

---

[18] Lee Hardy, *The Fabric of this World: Inquiries into Calling, Career Choice, and the Design of Human Work* (Grand Rapids: Eerdmans, 1990).

resurrection). If our work really does form and express at least a part of our human identity and personality, and since this work is genuinely now a part of the physical creation, it is not then unwarranted to think that, along with resurrecting us, God can "resurrect" some of these things too. It is obviously impossible to illustrate here how each of the innumerable forms of human work will survive. Our example of the wheel serves only to set the course for each of us to imaginatively hope, or suppose, how each of our activities (even the most transient ones) will be gathered up and transformed.

But how does all of this apply to our imaging God presently, with the judgements that we are called to make now about what we do in our work and how we go about doing it? Can our judgements really image God as anticipations of God's judgement such that we can be working co-operatively with him in the present?

Why not? This is the pattern that has emerged throughout our study. As God's working apprentices, surely we can and should exercise our freedom and responsibility in our choice of work and in the way we work. In a completely fallen condition and without God it would be impossible to image God in this way. Yet now that we are spiritual ("in Christ" by the power of the Spirit) we are freed and enabled, as 1 Corinthians 2:15 tells us, to make "judgements about all things."

So what might this look like in our working lives? First, we will need to gain some personal distance from that which relentlessly occupies us – our work. This does not mean that we divorce our work completely from our identity, but rather that we find some healthy space so that we can distinguish between the whole picture of who we are and our specific occupational activities.

This self-judgement is crucial. Yet to engage in it we will need a vantage point from which to examine honestly and carefully who we have become (our gifts and our deepest desires), and whether our current occupation (or a future one), as structured and practiced in a particular culture, is the most appropriate outlet for us to creatively image God within this creation. In all of this, too, we need to keep an eye on the coming new creation.

It is exciting to realize that this vantage point is precisely what Sabbath is all about, and what it makes possible. It is a regular time and space, as well as a perspective, from which to make these necessary judgements. Weekly church life at its best will give us some opportunity to have a Sabbath rest and, with each helping the other, to reflect upon who we are and are becoming, our gifts, our desires, our opportunities, and work. Through worship together, we discern a "God's-eye" perspective. Church should form, train, and liberate us to be the judges of "all things" (1 Cor. 2:15). Sabbath is not, then, the end of a week's work. Christians celebrate Sabbath on Sunday, the first day of the week. Sabbath for Christians includes a rest, but it is also the starting point from which an increasingly Christ-shaped working week can flow.

Clearly, then, our calling to judge all things applies to how we embody, shape, and carry out our work, as well as, to the degree that our circumstances allow, to what we choose to do as our work. With the help of other Christians who know and love us, we are called to make spiritual judgements about whether the career or job that we seek or have is, or can be to some degree, characterized by the four-fold nature of salvation found in the new heaven and new earth that we saw in Chapter 3. In order to discern this we need to ask some searching questions.

Does, or can, this or that occupation allow me to work as God's apprentice according to his purpose for this creation?

Given the ambiguities and ambivalence in this specific work, does it (or how can it) in some measure promote and build harmonious relationships between God and humanity, between people, and between people and nature?

Does this work promote or contribute to the psychological wholeness and flourishing of people in themselves?

Is this work suited to who I am and am becoming with my gifts and talents?

Does (or how can) this work and its results allow me and others to flourish as God's apprentices?

How can we together, with the help of God's Spirit, minimize or even eliminate its hindering us from this purpose?

Working through questions like these is what it means for God's people to spiritually judge all things. Having the freedom and maturity to continually make, and to get better at making, these judgements is a significant part of what our spirituality of work is about. Although this process might lead from time to time to making hard decisions, and even to frustration concerning what to work at or how best to work, at least this frustration will be a healthy one if we rely more and more on God as we seek to image him in our daily work.

Yet is such liberation to purposeful work really what it means to do spiritual work, or rather, to work spiritually? Is this really what so much of the life of faith is supposed to be about? If it is, many of us feel like we are a long way from such a spirituality of work and church experience.

Faith beyond Mere Obedience

Once, when I was a guest preacher in a Sunday morning worship service, I had just finished speaking on the heavenly good of earthly work and had come to the amen of the closing prayer. Obviously feeling that he could contain his anger no longer, an extremely irate man broke the silence just then and began loudly, with much hostility, to attack my theological understanding of work. I had been reflecting on the idea that our spiritual motivation in our ordinary work surely included, but also went well beyond, doing it simply out of obedience to God. I had suggested, for example, that another equally proper motivation for work was to love and serve our neighbor. But even this, I reflected, as obviously biblical as it was, is not the final word.

In the sermon I had unpacked the vision that our work, once transformed through judgement, would provide some of the building materials that God will use in the construction of the new earth. Then I explored how we are therefore free to understand and experience our work as a genuine co-operation with God – not just for the here and now, but also for shaping eternity.

In order to illustrate this point I had recounted how a good friend and colleague had been in prison for his faith during the Soviet period in Ukraine. It was common for the guards, as a form of psychological torture, to require prisoners to undertake the most menial and laborious work possible. So, for example, guards would have prisoners move huge piles of rubble from one side of the camp to the other. When they had finished, the guards would then command that they move it back again. Thus although the work was excruciatingly difficult, the most painful part was that it was utterly meaningless since in the end it accomplished nothing.

The purpose of the illustration was to help the congregation probe more deeply into their feelings and beliefs. Do we as Christians sometimes think of, and even experience, our daily work and relationship to God in a similar way? Most of us struggle at times with the sinking feeling that what we work at daily really helps no one. While this is probably not strictly true, it is particularly difficult to see the truth if we are already frustrated with our work. Likewise, we often believe that our work accomplishes very little, if anything, in terms of eternally important matters. Yet God requires that we still do it, we reason, even though it will all burn up in the end. God doesn't require judgement on our part, only obedience.

I developed this particular sermon illustration even further. Since, I reasoned, we know that God is *not* like the Soviet prison guard, he is *not* a sadistic torturer of the people he rules, we are therefore justified in enquiring about the deeper meaning of our work. Since we have faith in a God whose love for his people never changes, we can trust that his commands, including his "command" to work, is not like the prison guard's that tells us to do something as a punishment or knowing that it is ultimately meaningless. Thus, since God is *not* arbitrary in his mandates, we are more than just "allowed" to look for the deeper and lasting meaning bound up with his command that we work. Because of God's nature, a search for such meaning should become an integral part of every Christian's deepening spiritual walk with him. Spiritual maturity is all about making such judgements.

As reasonable as this thinking seemed to me and most others in the congregation, it did not seem that way at all to this man. His angry retort was that we should do work, and everything else God has instituted, simply because he commands us to. According to him, no deeper judgement is possible, and no deeper meaning is to be sought, since to do so would be to question God. Simple and humble obedience, he was trying angrily to express, is its own reward and thus the goal and the purpose of the Christian life. Obedience alone is the sign of, and way to, spiritual maturity.

But his vision of the spiritual life doesn't reflect the theology and spirituality of work we have seen. Of course the call to obediently serve God and our neighbor's needs is bound up with human purpose and our personal relationship with God. Such work is our primary way of loving both God and others and of taking care of this creation. Yet we need to decide, to judge as God calls us to, whether our work itself (and how carry it out) indeed shows this love to God and others as we hope. "Obediently" producing things or states of affairs that in fact destroy people and the environment can hardly mean loving and serving God, even if in the process we pray for success, are quite kind and compassionate to our employees, and accept this work as providentially given by God. We need to exercise deeper judgement and seek a broader vision if we want to image God in our work. To truly "obey" God's call requires much more than a simple acquiescence and internal disposition of piety.

On an individual level, for example, we may feel that we are expressing our faithfulness to God, accepting his providential guidance, by working in that factory where he has us and making the highest quality pesticides that our giftedness and training allow. But if these pesticides are shown on balance to hurt people and nature, maybe we are not being as obedient as we might initially think. Discernment is required.

Partnering with God

In harmony with what we have seen so far within our theology, and in order to reflect more deeply from Scripture on the implications of these reflections on the spirituality of work, we bring this chapter to a close by briefly considering two additional biblical texts. First we will look at a few of Jesus' words in the Gospel of John. Then we will return to the section of Romans 8 that we passed over in Chapter 3.

In John 15:14–15 Jesus explains the kind of relationship he intends to have with us. It may surprise some to find that what Jesus, the Lord of the universe, desires of us is friendship rather than servitude. We are his friends (in a right relationship with him), he says, if we do what he "commands" – that is, if we love each other (Jn. 15:10, 12, 14). But what is the nature of this obedience?

Obedience is, of course, central to Christian spirituality. However, Jesus does not allow us to read any worldly meaning into the notion of obedience. As he explains his vision for our lives, what he says in verse 14 (that we *are* his friends), and in verse 15 (that *he* no longer calls us servants), turns on its head what most would expect obedience to him to mean. Jesus' subversion of standard definitions of obedience means that we should not think of our relationship with him in terms of blind servitude. Rather, his desire for us as friends goes much deeper.

A servant does not know the deeper aspects of his master's business (v. 15). Nor would a slave worker see the bigger picture. A genuine friend, however, does know his friend's business. Being a "servant" *may* be a starting point in our relationship with Christ, but the goal of friendship requires that we grasp the deeper purposes and dimensions of *his* ways just as he searches and intimately know us and our ways.

With this counter-intuitive understanding of obedience as friendship, it is spiritually inappropriate to settle for a relationship with God characterized by subservience, or what we might call unquestioning obedience. Rather, "in Christ" even in this life we have been let in on the secret of God's purposes, on why God made us and where creation will end up.

A parallel biblical notion to that in John 15 is that when we are "in Christ" we become, together with Jesus, "sons" of God. In Romans 8:13–17 Paul explains that living by the Spirit makes us children of God rather than his fearful slaves. Although he often refers to himself as a slave of Christ, what Paul says in this passage suggests that he means something quite different from what we might commonly expect.

Romans 8:15 says, "For you did not receive a spirit that makes you a slave again to fear, but you received the Spirit of sonship. And by him we cry '*Abba*, Father.' " Our relationship to God is open and personal. This is not a relationship of subjugation to a far-off master; it does not exclude human initiative or co-operation through personal judgements. Rather, our understanding of obedience to God needs to be reinterpreted according to the notion of sonship.

Verse 17 presents the most amazing idea. We are not children of God in the sense that we simply do what he says. We are more. We are heirs of God and co-heirs with Christ. We are not called sub-heirs; we are not subordinated to Jesus in any way. Rather, living "in Christ" by the Spirit means that we have an equal share in everything that belongs to Christ. And, since Christ is God as well as human, what is God's is now ours. We are "heirs of God." As we have seen, Christ's glorification is our glorification.

In terms of our work, this notion of sonship together with co-heirship is significant. Given this spiritual status, we cannot be thought of as sub-workers with God. We are now, and forever will be, genuinely God's co-workers (and co-heirs) with more freedom and more status than even the first Adam had.

This passage suggests that, in Christ, the apprentices have now become full members of the guild, qualified masters in our own right. Of course, we are not yet fully partakers in this divine nature, so humility while we await "graduation" is still required. Indeed, even though we are masters in this life, we are still going to get many things wrong and need *the* Master of masters to guide us.

The point of this passage, however, is to be freeing rather than humiliating. We are not slaves – in this life or in the next. We are not ignorant of the deeper meaning and purpose of what we are to be about or do within God's kingdom. Rather, "in Christ" even in this life we have been let in on the secret of God's purposes, on how and why God does things the way he does. We have been brought into the dynamic kingdom reality that faith begins with, but then goes much further than, obedience. If we are subservient or ignorant of God's ways and kingdom values, then we are not genuine friends with Christ, children of God, or mature Christians.

If in the new creation everything that is Christ's finally and completely becomes ours (and everything that is ours becomes his), then we have the "right" even now to judge all things. That is, we have the right to *seek* to understand how what we are doing in this life, including our ordinary work, fulfils God's purpose – even if our understanding of this now will always be less than perfect. Being a co-worker with Christ means something both now and in eternity.

Some might object to the idea of the heavenly good of earthly work on the grounds that it overestimates the value of human work and suggests that we are far more important than we could ever be in the grand scheme of things. My response is simply that Jesus' aspirations for us were far greater than maybe ours are for ourselves. Paul's understanding is that our glorification and adoption ensure that we, too, have all the insider rights of Christ. Surely, having seen the importance God places on work, this includes the right to see and appreciate the place and value of our work in the light of eternity.

6

Shaping the Things to Come: Mission for the Masses

Jesus said to them, "My Father is always at his work to this very day, and I, too, am working . . . I tell you the truth, the Son can do nothing by himself; he can do only what he sees his Father doing, because whatever the Father does the Son also does."

John 5:17, 19–20

"I tell you the truth, anyone who has faith in me will do what I have been doing. He will do even greater things than these, because I am going to the Father." *John 14:12*

Times had changed. It was January 1991, the wall had come down, and it was an exciting time to be a missionary in the USSR. Since there were not yet many of us there from the west, the sense of adventure was breathtaking. Our spiritual optimism was swelling. God had brought us here, the advance guard for a western (and eastern, often Korean as it would turn out) missionary force that would soon follow. We felt as if we were riding on the crest of a tidal wave from the Holy Spirit and there was no telling what amazing things God was going to do in that land through us.

I was hopeful. I had a seminary degree and plenty of resources, since it was not difficult back then to raise financial support in America for missionary work behind the Iron Curtain, in the heart of the "evil empire." What perfect timing. We were ready, financially resourced, and there was a real spiritual hunger among the people. I was sure that, by God's grace, we would soon be making a real "kingdom" difference as missionaries in Moscow. Soon, wave after wave of missionaries – both residential and "missionary tourists" (who came for short visits with no knowledge of the culture, language or history) – did come to what, by the end of that year, were the countries of the former Soviet Union.

So what happened? Why didn't things work out as well as we had hoped? Why did so much of our ministry seem to go nowhere, even as the reports back home kept saying that thousands upon thousands were coming to faith in our evangelistic rallies? Why did the gospel we presented seem to inoculate so many against real faith? We found, for example, long-standing churches splitting around us – and often suggesting that we had been the catalyst. The more humble ministries of many national believers couldn't compete with our flashy events, steady financial resources, our methods, media and sophistication.

I suppose I can see, in hindsight, that God did use who we were and what we did to help quite a few people personally. God is good that way. He can take almost anything we offer and make something out of it for his purposes. And besides, we did do a few things well – I think.

Yet for me and many of my colleagues, during that enormous missionary onslaught to Russia, a crisis deep within the modern "faith missions movement" was further exposed. What scared us was that it seemed to go deeper than most of us had realized. I say further exposed because, as we knew from the experiences of many others, there had been cracks and warnings for decades. Yet, for some reason, we were sure that this time things would be different. After all, some of us had at least studied the stories of our missionary forefathers and knew the pitfalls to watch for.

Yet within a decade after missionary activity began in the former Soviet Union, a number of us would find ourselves, along with a growing number of faith missionaries working around the world, compelled to rethink our whole understanding of the missionary enterprise – and, even more importantly, the theology that lay behind it.

In Moscow, some of us had begun to worship with and serve as missionaries alongside Soviet-era believers and a growing number of new converts. These were wonderful folk, struggling like we all were to understand the implications of this seismic political shift for life in general, and for the kingdom of God in particular. And it was all quite exciting at first, even though at times, and for reasons I couldn't totally figure out, I felt a little uncomfortable about being there as a "missionary."

However, it didn't take all that long before several of us began to feel very uneasy about how things were developing. Each week another missionary like me, or yet another missionary tourist, would visit our worship service and, as was the local custom, be given a slot to "say a few words," or preach. Some weeks there were so many visitors that our pastor, a wonderful Ukrainian man with a real pastor's heart and deep wisdom concerning what his people were facing, was himself left with no time to address us. We were simply overrun by missionaries.

But this was not in itself the real problem. Visiting missionary after visiting missionary would stand up and preach about the exciting evangelistic/missionary opportunities now open to those fortunate enough to have the free time and financial resources to take advantage of them. But, again and again, we heard the same people offer similar words of "testimony" about how they came to Russia: "I'm not sure why God called me here. I have no specific training for this context or knowledge of your church, culture, or language. But isn't it amazing that God would call an ordinary person like me, release me from the daily grind of my meaningless (but well-paying) job back home, provide me with plenty of money, and send me here to be a missionary to spread the gospel?" As a recruiting advertisement in America for one prominent missionary initiative claimed, "If you can press the button on a VCR you are halfway there."

I am not exaggerating. Week after week we heard this same message, including, in some form or another, the denigration of "meaningless" ordinary work. People "preached" it from the front at worship and shared it with us during the week when we saw them in Moscow's McDonald's or met with them while our Russian friends were at work.

A taskforce of traveling evangelists, residential short- and long-term "friendship evangelists," and church planters had indeed arrived. But was this really a good thing? Was this what missionary work was supposed to be about? Something was clearly not right. Lives and livelihoods were crumbling around us as government-based employment and welfare systems, the only ones there were, fell apart. How did the gospel really relate to life? The message of salvation we presented through our work as "friendship evangelists" began to sound more and more shallow – like a denunciation of daily life and a form of escapism.

If people couldn't quite see how our message provided escape, they thought perhaps making friends with a westerner would provide that for them. "Maybe our missionary friends can get us out of here if we respond to their message? Maybe my missionary friend will get me out of here if I become increasingly like her, imitating her Christian ways?"

I'm not being cynical about this, nor do I blame our rather desperate and suffering friends for seeking a way out. Yet the phenomenon of "rice Christians" wasn't new, and we should have been ready for it. But could we have been prepared? Or was what we preached and modeled as missionaries guaranteed to produce them?

"Rice Christians" aside, it didn't take long for our mature Russian Christian friends to catch on to our spirituality and theology of mission. Often we would have conversations in which people would ask us whether we thought that, when they grew enough spiritually (implying "when I become as spiritual as you are"), God would call them into the ministry so that they could engage in his work.

They made it perfectly clear to us that we had set before them the goal. To them we were modeling what it meant to be "spiritual" and a real missionary. But was this really what it means to do God's work? Was this really a theology of mission that they could live with, or were we simply embodying beliefs and piety that would lead them to spiritual, rather than just political, frustration? To this day, many of these folk are still waiting and wondering if eventually God might call them to leave their work and become missionaries.

A Theology of Mission for the Rest of Us

These experiences working as a traditional missionary in Russia and Ukraine largely sparked my personal journey into exploring the theology and spirituality of work. Let's look now at a few of the implications of what we have explored: What does it mean to be a "real" missionary?

A lot of the spiritual frustration that ordinary working Christians experience boils down to feelings that they are cut off from, and only indirectly involved with, God in his real mission in the world. This is why it is essential for our churches to develop and embody a more theologically robust, practical, and spiritually liberating understanding of missions that incorporates at its core the whole life and work of every believer.

Believers desperately need to grasp why and how mission is what they, the whole people of God, are engaged in already while at work. More specifically, they need to grasp why and how the work *itself* that we do is missionary activity rather than just an occasion for it. So what does a theology of mission based on the heavenly good of earthly work that is suited to ordinary working Christians look like?

The theology and spirituality we have examined have enormous implications for mission. Clearly, we need to think again about what a missionary is. For we have seen that, when done in a way that images God and thus co-operates with him, human work *in itself* is Christian missionary activity. Why? *Because it is largely (though not exclusively) through our work that we reflect God's image and co-operate with him in bringing people and the whole creation to humanity's and nature's ultimate maturity and future.* Our work, as we have seen, is at the core of God's purpose for our existence and our salvation. We are saved to become together the image of Christ, and thus the image of God – and we express and develop this most directly in our work.

Negatively, this means that any understanding of mission that fails to grasp that *in itself* human work is fundamental to God's purpose (the mission of God or kingdom of God) for us and creation will be theologically flawed. Likewise, missions thinking that fails to incorporate this theology ultimately undermines the missionary calling of the people of God. For the majority of Christians simply cannot now, nor could they ever, measure up to the modern faith missionary ideal of leaving home and work "to work" for God. For what that understanding of mission unintentionally does is marginalize and thus alienate the vast majority of Christians in the world who will spend most of their lives and life's energy in ordinary work.

In this final chapter, then, we offer a new theology of mission that reflects the heavenly good of earthly work. Although we cannot fully develop this in one chapter, the material based on our discussion thus far will provide plenty of avenues for future explorations into this new theology of mission.

While I offer this challenge to missions in general, many before me have recognized that the modern missionary movement faces a crisis. Most evangelical leaders acknowledge that the western mission enterprise is in trouble and that something is fundamentally wrong with the "faith missions movement." David Bosch's now classic *Transforming Mission* can in many ways be said to have set the agenda and opened the floodgate for a lot of new thinking about what mission is and what it means to be a missionary.[19]

Two more recent books also deserve brief consideration here because they take up the challenge to recast our theology

[19] David Bosch, *Transforming Mission: Paradigm Shifts in Theology of Mission* (Maryknoll, NY: Orbis, 1991).

(including our understanding of the meaning of salvation) and to radically alter the way we view and carry out the missionary enterprise. These are *Changing the Mind of Missions: Where Have We Gone Wrong*? by James Engel and William Dyrness and *Mission after Christendom* by David Smith.[20]

Engel and Dyrness argue that the modern western missionary movement is fundamentally compromised because of its dependence upon modernity, and particularly upon modern western political and economic power structures. The movement is flawed, as is its theology, because of its grounding and ideological basis in, and its dependence upon, both western democratic thinking and surplus or disposable cash.

Indeed, this is what I finally came to understand so painfully in Russia. What we were proclaiming as the message of salvation and what we were modeling as missionary activity were shaped by, and dependent upon, certain western ideals: a culturally conditioned and individualistic concept of salvation; the political guarantee of religious freedom; and the steady flow of surplus funds to free people from the "daily grind of work" to enable them to become missionaries and spread this gospel.

For obvious theological and practical reasons, the western missions movement needs to free itself from this dependency. Theologically, it is satisfying to see that the theology of work reflecting the heavenly good of earthly work provides a way forward. It allows us to tell the story of salvation in a way that makes room for each person but is not individualistic. That is, it builds from our hope for a future bodily resurrection, but sees this by definition as including our communities, cultures and even our natural environment. It therefore suggests a new understanding of missionary activity – one that embraces our material existence and physical life as eternally important.

---

20 James F. Engel and William A. Dyrness, *Changing the Mind of Missions: Where Have We Gone Wrong*? (Downers Grove, IL: IVP, 2000), and David Smith, *Mission After Christendom* (London: Darton, Longman & Todd, 2003).

Every Christian at work, school, or in the home can co-operate with God in their daily work, and thus in their work *itself* they can become missionaries. (And, as we will soon see, this inclusive vision of mission applies equally to those whose personal faith journeys have not yet even brought them to the point of full belief.)

By simply working toward, and along with, the "kingdom values" we saw expressed in the four-fold meaning of salvation, all people, whether they realize it or not, are working with God toward his mission and purposes. Neither political freedom nor financial freedom is required to be this kind of missionary.

Logistically speaking, our theology of the heavenly good of earthly work provides a way forward for the missionary movement that increasingly in the west, but also in most other places in the world, finds that the financial resources for a full-blown "faith mission" enterprise are simply not there. In other words, given growing world economic realities, "pay as you go missions" through ordinary work will be the only future for the vast majority of Christians, and especially for those coming from poorer countries.

As important as this is, my greater concern is still theological. For bad theology ultimately won't work, regardless of its logistical by-products. And here again, while discussing the characteristics of "kingdom mission," Engel and Dyrness helpfully outline five qualities of mission that clearly dovetail with our reflections on the heavenly good of earthly work.[21] It is worth quoting these at length, for what they say reflects so well this theology and spirituality of work:

> Christian witness emanates, as it should, from the grassroots outward through a community of believers whose corporate life consistently bears the fruit of the Spirit, thereby providing an authentic and winsome embodiment of the gospel;

[21] Engel and Dyrness, *Changing the Mind of Missions*, 94–95.

> Seeds are planted and brought into life as ordinary people follow the model of their Lord in daily life, always seeking to provide a reason for the hope that is within them;
>
> Believers function as true pilgrims, inviting the lost to join them on a journey as part of a community of pilgrims who have found hope;
>
> This witness, while small and almost indiscernible, grows in power and impact as a single point of light expands into multiple points of light;
>
> Outcomes are assessed by discernible changes in individual lives, in society and in the church.

Engel and Dyrness do not offer these reflections on mission with an eye to our daily work as missionary activity. Yet it is hard to imagine how all of God's people could embody characteristics like these unless they were grounded in a theology of work. Mission like this could only become a reality for the whole people of God with a deeper root and branch rethink of theology that places ordinary work *at the center* of missionary activity.

This concern leads us to consider the insights of another contemporary European thinker on mission. David Smith has grasped that an even deeper and more profound change in thinking is required within western theology and western concepts of mission if the missionary enterprise is to survive. Although his concern is similar to that of Engel and Dyrness in *Changing the Mind of Missions*, in *Mission after Christendom* Smith urges a wholesale rethinking of the theology that has so overwhelmingly shaped our missionary practice.

Smith argues, and rightly so, that most western theology was shaped by and embodies the ideal and conditions of a "western Christendom" that no longer exists. His point is that we need to embrace rather than lament this, and change the way we formulate and embody our beliefs. As we come to see our own blind spots, with the help of this cultural change and by exploring Christian theology developed in different cultural contexts, we should be in a better position to reform our beliefs and practice to reflect God and his ways more faithfully.

Theology, of course, shouldn't change simply to "keep up with the times" or so that Christians can try to be "relevant" and just like our changing world. Good theology does not fold to fads or trends in this way but will always seek genuinely to correspond to the way God and things really are. It will always seek to be faithful to Scripture and grounded in the tradition of which it is a part.

Yet as good theology fulfils its purpose – that is, as it helps us to interpret our world and live life prophetically in order to bring about godly change in ever fluid cultural contexts – it inevitably will pose a host of new questions. Christians continually engaging in the theological task will thus come to see new things in the Bible and in tradition and will gain new insights into life that others – in different times and places, and asking different questions – will have missed.

Along these lines, what Smith quite brilliantly offers us is a description and analysis of western culture, together with fresh readings of several biblical texts, that together highlight the challenges that theology, and the missions enterprise, face today. He builds his reflections around three shifts that he shows to be taking place in western culture, and indeed in the current world order. These are secularization, pluralization, and globalization.

Our theology and spirituality of work, then, dovetails with and addresses our emerging world context. In particular, we have reflected on the centrality of ordinary work to: 1) God's final purposes; 2) the vision of heaven and the future new creation; 3) Jesus' person and work as the paradigm for creation's salvation; 4) God's original design of, and intention for, creation; 5) humanity and human purpose; and 6) the scope of salvation and the value of the material creation as bound up with, and equal to, spiritual reality. Each of these doctrines offers a window into, and a hope for, a secularized, pluralized and globalized world.

So in a pluralized world, for example, where experimental spiritualities are becoming increasingly trendy and common, especially in the workplace, Christians need to offer a spirituality and a spiritual vision that integrates who we are and what we do in life and work with deeper questions about personal and physical existence. In a secularized world where the marketplace increasingly sets the agenda and determines cultural values and goals, Christians need to embody with their work and in their ways of working the goals and values that characterize and point to the present and coming kingdom of God. In a globalized world where our working activities show the interconnectedness and interdependence of different peoples around the world, as well as the relationship people have with the world itself, Christians through their work need to develop ever better ways to care for and empower others and the rest of creation to flourish. The final story at the end of this chapter offers one example of what this looks like for the ordinary working Christian.

As we have seen, these missionary – or what we might better call "missional" – activities are integral to God's purposes for us and the world. Thus work is not a platform for mission or evangelism, as if it were somehow subordinate to salvation and eternity. Rather, godly work itself actually spreads, by embodying God's good news, a present experience and foretaste of salvation. For work in itself is a genuine form of life imaging God. It is an ever-open invitation to all to co-operate with God in his purposes.

A New Kind of Missionary

Given this theology, mission and missionary activity can no longer be understood as a specialized task for a few specifically called professionals. *Mission is the work (God's work) for everyone created to be in God's image and indeed therefore for the whole people of God.*

The thrust of this idea is not new, of course. Mission specialists have been saying similar things for decades to try to mobilize Christians, congregations, and denominations to give, pray, send, and go. What is new in terms of the heavenly good of earthly work, however, is that the converse is also true. Although work is not the sum total of God's purpose for us, it is nonetheless true that: *Work is the mission (God's mission) for everyone created to be in God's image and indeed therefore for the whole people of God.*

What changes with this definition of mission is our perception of *who* in actual fact has a working focus on "spiritual things," and thus of who is a "genuine" and full-time missionary. Our new theological view of work no longer allows us to regard what we traditionally call "religious work" as the only spiritual work that impacts eternity. As a result of this, many of us who are used to seeing things and living the other way will need to make a seismic shift in the way we live our Christian life. For what this means is that most, if not all, of the world is already filled with God's missionaries. Unfortunately most of us have failed to recognize this and to reorient our whole lives, ordinary and religious, accordingly.

Many Christian traditions have been probing toward something like this for quite a long time. I say probing, for most often we have not integrated our belief that Christians are called to be salt and light in the workplace with what we believe and practice concerning "real" missions. Yet the Spirit has a way of breaking through, whether our theology has made space for him or not. So it isn't uncommon to hear someone say to those out in the marketplace that they really are God's representatives. Indeed they are.

Yet, more often than not, this comes across as somewhat patronizing to working people. This is because our practice of church, our spiritual heroes, and our beliefs about spiritual/eternal things have spoken louder than our words and have undermined what we might have intended. It's not that we don't mean what we say. But usually we intend something like, "Your work is of a great deal of earthly good and we're glad you're out there, for all of our sakes. And it might even give you opportunities, on the side, to evangelize and thus do something really important."

So our words ring hollow when we only regularly and publicly pray for those missionaries on "faith support." And it is hard to believe that we really are full-time "salt and light" when only visiting missionaries are asked to come up front in church and visit our small groups to talk about the ups and downs of their ministries.

If the theology of mission incorporating the heavenly good of earthly work is on the right track, Christians, congregations, and denominations need to do the following: 1) learn how better to recognize this larger missionary force for what it really is; 2) acknowledge the heavenly value of work's spiritual/physical ministry; and 3) direct more of our corporate energies to empowering this whole missionary taskforce. Although each of us can start where we are, what will be required to bring about the needed shift to this new ethos is larger than any of us alone could accomplish.

So how could we work together toward this vision? Mostly we need to practice. Slow and steady will win the race. When we are together in our various Christian gatherings and meetings, small or large, formal and informal, we have to be intentional about devising ways to help us see each person in their daily work as a missionary. This means that we, like the new Adams we are in Christ, need to consciously practice bearing God's image by continually "naming" ourselves and our work as missionary. And if we are actually going to get beyond seeing work or the marketplace as a platform for "real" spiritual ministry, we will probably have to overdo this for a while.

We will have to teach ourselves to tell the gospel story along the lines we have explored. Telling our own life story in this way, for example in a time set aside for sharing or testimony, would be a good way to start. We can also use the material in this book for Bible study or times of meditation to help us to see how the gospel story and the stories of our own daily lives mesh together. Through regular and focused study and meditation we will come to a deeper understanding of the relationship between Christ's work as imaging God and our work as imaging God. And we will see more and more clearly how both fit together in the Triune God's larger purposes to bring creation to its intended goal.

Naturally, we will have to practice thinking about having Christ-like *attitudes* at specific times or with particular people in our work. We will also need to stretch our imaginations, sometimes to the point of breaking, so that we can experiment together – envisioning how this or that specific task or job *in fact* works according to God's four-fold salvation and how it might find a transformed place in eternity. And if, after sustained reflection, we become convicted that our specific work in this or that industry simply doesn't meet the criteria of pointing to God's four-fold salvation (and thus doesn't co-operate appropriately with God), then we need to practice together envisioning how we as individuals and communities might help each other to find new work in another industry. So, for example, it might not take much to convince someone in the sex industry (a porn film maker), or a dealer in illegal drugs, to see that their work is not in line with a kingdom vision of human flourishing, community health, and spiritual renewal. But what about work in what some would see as grey areas – for example in the military or nuclear industry, or in aspects of the entertainment industry such as breweries, or in the design, production, and selling of violent video games or movies? Here we might conclude that it is better to remain in an industry so that we can facilitate change within it, and thus society. To enable such cutting-edge mission, believers will also need to practice together envisioning how we as individuals and communities might bring such change about. Of course, this depends upon the degree to which we have such influence.

Yet nobody is without some level of influence in a working environment, whether at the structural level or even on a smaller personal scale.

Further, we will also want to be more focused and careful in our Christian gatherings to pray purposely for each other with regard to the specific work/mission related issues we face. We will want to pray not just that our colleagues come to faith, but also that the job we are currently working on might reflect God and his ways (God's kingdom) as we serve others and creation. We will need to offer up each other's work to God in prayer and then be there to help each other work through the difficulties and challenges we face daily in our mission. We will likewise celebrate and praise God together over work well done or work that seems to be going well.

Although putting these suggestions into practice may feel awkward at first, and even somewhat artificial or clumsy, over time this reorientation will become a natural part of who we are and of our life together. After all, children only learn to use language and thus shape their world by speaking – and it takes a lot of practice.

Yet as important as this focus is on what we can do as Christians gathered together, if we are not careful we could bog ourselves down yet again in church-based programs and activities rather than putting the bulk of our energies into the mission itself. Of course, worship is its own end. It is not just or primarily about training for life and service. But so much of what we do at church seems to be about the institution of the church, and that is worrying.

There is a further and deeper danger that this focus on what *we as Christians* can do together could lead to exclusivity – unless we are careful to keep God's mission, rather than the church, at the center. Indeed, in this new understanding of mission, all people, whether Christian or not, have this calling – humanity was created to be in God's image – and thus can find a place in work within God's mission. Of course, in Christ we are the first fruits of salvation and in this sense have sojourned further in our spiritual journeys toward the world's final destiny. Thus, being Christians and enabled by the Spirit's filling, we should become "salt and light" in a special way within God's mission. Yet this should not blind us to the fact that God's purposes are for everyone – his is a universal kingdom.

Although this might sound quite radical at first, it's actually not when we think about it. All people were created to image God, and thus all people by virtue of their humanity are included in God's purposes for creation. Not all people image God in fellowship with him, but we do nevertheless corporately carry out his mission to work in one way or another.

Importantly, our new mission enterprise based on the heavenly good of earthly work treats people differently from our old approach to mission. God still includes in his purposes those who haven't yet, haven't fully, or even won't ever, come to faith.

Previously, it was simple to categorize people sharply as either "them" or "us." In this way of thinking, the tendency was always to dehumanize others by treating "them" ultimately as projects. This, for example, is what full-time mission as "friendship evangelism" comes to ultimately – no matter how much we try to avoid it. Leading someone to the Lord often meant getting people to join up to Christianity, or to a particular church or denomination, getting them to "buy" our product, or getting them to sign on the dotted line with a prayer of repentance. If a person responds, they're in. But if they don't, then it is our "job" to move on to someone else.

With a new understanding of mission, however, the whole ethos is different. We come alongside those with whom we are already *interdependent* at work, helping to free them in the work they are already doing to embody ever more Christ-like work and thus progressively to reflect God in his intentions for the world. Of course, knowing early on that we don't have to justify ourselves through this work is vital, and proclaiming this in our work may be what attracts our co-workers toward God, or at least toward our spirituality, in the first place.

Further, God's mission to bring people in our whole lives (including in our work, which we are already doing) ultimately toward what we might call "real humanness" (Christ-likeness and thus God-likeness), when it is integrated with work is not something particularly religious or awkward. It is, rather, an open way for all of us to co-operate in work together. For non-believers it is an invitation to see what God's mission really is, the four-fold vision for salvation, and a way to bring them closer toward it in the way they work. A person can be moving toward this even before she might fully understand or believe. Someone on the way, on a daily spiritual journey in work, might find eventually that they have been drawn to this vision (which we have seen is the very person of Christ). They may, without even realizing it fully, be transformed through the process by God into someone new, and to a new way of being. Realizing that has been God's call all along is conversion.

Since this is a journey, some will not follow through to the end. Some will never come to full belief or full personal transformation. This is heartbreaking, but it is reality. Yet to the degree that even these folk in their work are swept along with us in our "heavenly" way of working, to the degree that their work in co-operation with us co-operates with the heavenly vision we are moving toward, they are still included and are participating in God's grace and mission. Whether they do this from their own spiritual centers, or because their particular work or working environment has been shaped by believers (and thus they are carried along), they will nonetheless be partners with us, and indeed with God. This is what Christians mean when they say that God is sovereign. Just by working, a person images God. The question is, as we saw in Genesis 1 – 11, whether they are doing so towards God's purposes and in right fellowship with him or not. And fellowship with God (either closer or more distant) is a step-by-step journey rather than an absolute "either-or." Even the daily life of a fully committed Christian attests to this.

Even though we are embodying it in a somewhat different way through work, this understanding of mission is actually not all that new. In fact, it dovetails nicely with what many of us have been discovering for a long time about mission. That is, people need to be included. They need to belong before they can believe. Whether it's the young person who comes to Christ on a summer missions trip, or the office worker who comes to faith after having been caught up in God's working purposes, the result is the same. Genuine belonging or inclusion most often precedes believing.

This observation is not a sell-out to some kind of cheap or easy grace. In fact, when we come to understand the spiritual journey in this way, as a way of discipleship, our reading of the gospels and of the experiences of Christ's closest followers begins to make a lot of sense. Christ included his disciples in his call to follow. Clearly, from the very start of their journeys, they were partners with Christ. He included them in his, and thus in the Father's, mission. The Gospels make it clear that this was the case before they fully believed, before they understood what really following Christ meant. What they knew was that the caller and the envisioned end were worth walking toward.

Rather than being misguided for inviting non-Christians to do God's work, our approach to mission is in fact Jesus' way – only lived out in the workplace. Jesus knew that people, by being created to image God together, long for connectedness and to belong to some purpose bigger than themselves. Once people see from the inside what Christ's way of being is all about, and that this is an authentic and holistic way of living and working, many will wholeheartedly enter into a deeper and fuller commitment. They will do this even though they will realize already that the way will be tough and full of struggle – the way of the cross.

Let me illustrate what I mean – unfortunately with a negative example. Once, in a church where I was working, a couple visited who had decided that they were interested in spiritual things. They weren't married but were living together as if they were. Neither came from religious or church backgrounds, but both felt hungry for something more. They wanted God in their lives. About this they were quite clear.

Both were professional musicians. So, the first thing they wanted to know was whether or not we had a choir that they could get involved in and contribute to. These weren't your average religious consumers; they genuinely wanted to get involved from the inside, and contribute something of who they were and what they did. Their hope was that, in the process, they would come to faith. They even said so – as well as they could without a developed "Christian language."

The problem, however, was that the choir director *rightly* saw the choir ministry as a spiritual work of leading the whole congregation in worship. I say this was a problem because, as he saw it, since these folk were not Christian, and since they were living in "sin," they could not join the choir. How could non-Christians "openly sinning" engage with Christians in spiritual work? They did not belong. They had not converted, and they were living together.

So, in the end, the decision was made that these people could not join the choir. So they went away – not "working" with us, and not, as far as I know, ever being brought to the faith and the Christ they were seeking.

Working in the Spirit: Mission that Works

Of course none of us, whether Christian or not, can genuinely image God in our work – or participate with God in his mission – without being enabled or gifted to do so by God the Spirit. A believer's inclusion "in Christ" (who is the fullness of God's image) is only accomplished, as we saw, by the Spirit. Thus a believer's inclusion in God's mission, and his or her ability to work co-operatively with God therein, must likewise be in, and by, the Spirit. It follows then that *work that is mission is work in the Spirit.*

But does this mean that the "natural" gifts and talents that we work with, those we seem to be born with and those we receive, discover, and develop throughout life are "spiritual" gifts? And, if so, are these "spiritual" in the same way, given by the Holy Spirit, as the "spiritual" gifts the Bible lists as given to the church?

Miroslav Volf, in his book *Work in the Spirit*, believes so and argues his case effectively.[22] To summarize, Volf argues that "As the firstfruits of salvation, the Spirit of Christ is not only active in the Christian fellowship but also desires to make an impact *on the world through* the fellowship."[23] Volf reminds us of Acts 2:17ff., where we find that the Spirit has now been poured out upon all flesh. This leads him to propose that "a person who is shaped by her genetic heritage and social interaction faces the challenge of a new situation as she lives in the presence of God and learns to respond in a new way. This is what it means to acquire a new spiritual gift".[24]

That this applies even to the workplace is clear, as long as we understand all of our new life in God's presence as life in the Spirit. So, the "spirit of God calls, endows, and empowers Christians to work in their various occupations."[25] "Even when *charisma* is exercised by using so called natural capacities, it would be incorrect to say that a person is 'enabled' irrespective of God's relation to him. Rather the enabling depends on the presence and activity of the Spirit."[26] Thus, as "Christians do their mundane work, the Spirit enables them to co-operate with God in the kingdom of God that 'completes creation and renews heaven and earth.' "[27]

But what about the work of non-believers? What about the gifts and talents they have? Do they come from God? Does the Spirit give these too? If so, are these "spiritual gifts"? As Volf argues:

---

22 Volf, *Work in the Spirit*, 111–19.

23 Volf, *Work in the Spirit*, 111 (emphasis his).

24 Volf, *Work in the Spirit*, 112.

25 Volf, *Work in the Spirit*, 113.

26 Volf, *Work in the Spirit*, 114.

27 Volf, *Work in the Spirit*, 115.

> All human work, however complicated or simple, is made possible by the operation of the Spirit of God in the working person; and all work whose nature and results reflect the value of the new creation is accomplished under the instruction and inspiration of the Spirit of God (see Isa. 28:24–29).[28]

It follows, then, that when "people work exhibiting the values of the new creation . . . then the Spirit works in them and through them."[29]

Indeed, Volf's conclusions merge with what we have seen already. With him, we would conclude, "To the extent that non-Christians are open to the prompting of the Spirit, their work, too, is the co-operation with God in anticipation of . . . the transformation of the world, even though they may not be aware of it."[30]

If, then, we want to be able to identify work in the Spirit we will need, as we have noted, to train our spiritual eyes to recognize work that participates with God in moving us and creation toward God's four-fold salvation. Again, these characteristics of God's kingdom are as follows: 1) a restored and flourishing personal relationship with God; 2) a restored and whole relationship with myself and a discovery of my true identity; 3) a restored and harmonious relationship between people; and 4) a harmonious relationship between people, nature, and God in which each is free to flourish as itself to the glory of God.

So what might work in the Spirit that corresponds to these four aspects of salvation look like? It would take many volumes even to begin to adequately reflect on this, but what follows are simply three ways that we might broadly recognize the Spirit "at work."

Work in the Spirit that is mission, or, mission that works will be work that preserves and maintains what is good in creation, both God-given and made by humanity.

---

28 Volf, *Work in the Spirit*, 114.

29 Volf, *Work in the Spirit*, 114.

30 Volf, *Work in the Spirit*, 119.

Work in the Spirit that is mission, or, mission that works will be work that clears away, as much as possible, those things that seek to confound the purposes of God and threaten to destroy his kingdom.

Work in the Spirit that is mission, or, mission that works will be work that produces new things that promote personal, communal, cultural, and environmental harmony and well-being – all in a restored relationship with God in Jesus Christ.

Work: Our Heavenly-Minded Mission

As we close, I want to illustrate what the vision of mission I am suggesting might look like at work. Doubtless a whole collection of stories like this, and from all spheres of working life, would be useful to help us train our imaginations to embrace mission that takes seriously the heavenly good of earthly work. Alas, this one story will have to suffice for now.

Jason works for a company that designs and manufactures specialized computer chips. His is a high-pressure job, but it isn't as exciting as some of the other jobs in the company. Neither is it the least exciting job, though he isn't directly involved in the more creative aspects of designing new products. Rather, Jason does the somewhat monotonous job in the lab of testing component parts, day in and day out, for the "brilliant" new chips that his colleagues, like Jack, have designed. He also has the tricky task of regularly explaining to the management chain that there is lots of testing to do, so they can't have an instant answer to "Does it work?"

Jack's work, in contrast, is exciting – and he loves it. He and his team get to create the chips that eventually make it into the latest technologies. His work gives him a buzz, and you might even say he is an adrenaline junky.

Jack takes most of his team's designs to Jason in the lab for testing. Even though there are several engineers in the department, over the last few years Jack has come to know and trust Jason. Of course, Jason is human and has his up and down days.

Nevertheless, over time Jack has noticed something different about Jason that draws him in. The best way he can describe it is that he is an authentic person and seems, despite the monotony and obvious frustration in his work, to find meaning within it. He treats it as more than just a way to get a wage.

The more Jack works with Jason, the more he begins subconsciously to adopt Jason's attitudes and ways of approaching work, as well as Jason's ways of working with people. Through this process, the hyper-competitive aspects of Jack's work, which have sustained him for so long, seem to be becoming slightly less central in his thinking. Something is happening to Jack that, at first, he doesn't even realize.

Somehow Jason's presence, and most probably a host of other things happening in Jack's life, brought Jack one Sunday afternoon to the place of questioning who he is and why he does the work that he does. Although the thrill of achievement and being successful has driven him and given him his identity for several years, he has now started to wonder whether this is what he wants his life to be about. He wonders: "Is this it?"

The next day at work Jason notices something different about Jack, and when Jack brings the next component to Jason for testing, Jason asks Jack if he is all right. A short conversation follows in which Jack raises the questions he is having about work.

A couple of weeks later Jack again brings some work to Jason. This time Jack asks Jason why he continues to work here and do a job that, frankly, is leading nowhere in terms of prestige and promotion and is so routinized that it would drive him crazy. Not wanting to sound "religious," but sensing the invitation to be honest, Jason tries to explain to Jack that he is not just working for himself, although given his personality he does find a degree of satisfaction in his work. Rather, Jason explains, he works with others and even with eternity in mind. As long as their company continues to drive technology forward and to make products that either directly or in some later-down-the-line application can be argued to make life better for others, he is happy to play his part and use his gifts and abilities in this work. Jason tells Jack that his work overall, though not in every way, helps him feel like he is, and can be, a part of what God is doing in the world, and a part of where God wants to take it.

At first Jack is blown away by this "spiritual" approach to work. But, reflecting later, he realizes that when he is around Jason he "picks up" and gets sucked into this same sense.

After some time Jack comes back to Jason, this time with a copy of the latest contract he and his team are to work on. He asks what Jason thinks about the intended use of the chip they are to design, and whether Jason thinks that this is the kind of thing he would be happy being a part of. Given its proposed immediate military use, Jason isn't at first sure how to respond. But, for his own sake and for Jack's, he would value spending some time together pondering and exploring this tricky question.

Jack admits to never having thought about his work this way, but he says that after their last conversation he can't help but do so now. Jack asks Jason if he might explore with him how their team might use their influence on those above to obtain more "meaningful" projects. Jack also asks if Jason might be willing to help him to understand more about the kind of beliefs that would suggest that somehow their projects could be part of God's purpose for the world . . .

For Further Reading

Badcock, Gary, *The Way of Life: A Theology of Christian Vocation* (Grand Rapids: Eerdmans, 1998).

Banks, Robert, *Faith Goes to Work: Reflections from the Marketplace* (Eugene, OR: Wipf & Stock, 1999).

Cosden, Darrell, *A Theology of Work: Work and the New Creation* (Paternoster Theological Monograph Series; Carlisle: Paternoster Press, 2004).

Greene, Mark, *Thank God It's Monday – Ministry in the Workplace* (London: Scripture Union, 2nd edn, 1997).

Hardy, Lee, *The Fabric of this World: Inquiries into Calling, Career Choice, and the Design of Human Work* (Grand Rapids: Eerdmans, 1990).

Larive, Armand, *After Sunday: A Theology of Work* (London and New York: Continuum, 2004).

Middleton, J. Richard, *The Liberating Image: The "Imago Dei" in Genesis 1* (Grand Rapids: Brazos Press, 2005).

Palmer, Parker J., *The Active Life: A Spirituality of Work, Creativity, and Caring* (San Francisco: Jossy-Bass Wiley, 1999).

Ryken, Leland, *Work and Leisure in Christian Perspective* (Eugene, OR: Wipf & Stock, 2002).

Stevens, R. Paul, *The Abolition of the Laity: Vocation, Work, and Ministry in Biblical Perspective* (Carlisle: Paternoster, 1999).

Veith, Gene E. Jr., *God at Work: The Spirituality of Ordinary Life* (Wheaton, IL: Crossway Books, 2002).

Volf, Miroslav, *Work in the Spirit: Toward a Theology of Work* (Eugene, OR: Wipf & Stock, 2001).